INTRODUCTION TO WOMEN'S STUDIES

About the Authors

Dr. Deepan Das, presently Assistant Professor of Political Science, R.G. Baruah College, Guwahati. He has completed his M.Phil. and Ph.D. from Dibrugarh University. He has published many books which are particularly meant for the students of political science. His area of interest is Government and Politics, Rural Development, Public Administration etc.

Dr. Tanusree Sarker, Associate Professor, Department of Political Science, Tinsukia Women's College. She has presented various research papers both in national and international seminars. Her area of interest is World Politics, Foreign Policy and Women's Studies.

Dr. Rakhimoni Gogoi, presently, Assistant Professor, Department of Political Science, Haflong Government College. She has completed her M.Phil. and Ph.D. from Dibrugarh University. Her area of interest is Public Administration, International Relations etc.

Introduction to Women's Studies

By
Dr. Deepan Das
Dr. Tanusree Sarker
Dr. Rakhimoni Gogoi

CONCEPT PUBLISHING COMPANY PVT. LTD.
NEW DELHI-110059

Introduction to Women's Studies: A book of Political Science for Three Year Degree (Semester System) Course prepared as per new Semester Syllabus of Dibrugarh University for 6th semester written by Dr. Deepan Das, Astt. Prof., Deptt. of Political Science, R.G. Baruah College, Dr. Tanusree Sarker, Associate Professor, Deptt. of Political Science, Tinsukia Women's College, Tinsukia and Dr. Rakhimoni Gogoi, Astt. Prof. Deptt. of Political Science, Haflong Government College and Published by Concept Publishing Company Pvt. Ltd., New Delhi.

BOOK CODE-AS-1

ISBN-13: 978-93-86682-83-6 (HB)
ISBN-13: 978-93-86682-85-7 (PB)

First Published 2019

Published and Printed by

Concept
Since 1974

Concept Publishing Company Pvt. Ltd.
A/15-16, Commercial Block, Mohan Garden,
New Delhi-110059 (INDIA)
T: 91 11 25351460, 91 11 25351794
E: publishing@conceptpub.com; *W*: www.conceptpub.com

Preface

Women's Studies, an interdisciplinary academic discipline is comparatively a new subject that delves on various feminist perspectives. This academic field explores politics, society and history from intersectional, multicultural women's perspectives. Women's Studies were first emerged as an academic discipline in the later part of 1970 in the USA. The courses of Women's Studies became available in the late 20th century at many colleges and universities around the world. Women's Studies encompass the deconstruction of traditional disciplines in terms of their subject matter and their structure. It is not limited solely to women's issues but various forms of oppressions in which women's issues become intricate focal points. It also includes the basic concepts of women's studies as gender, patriarchy and socialization.

This book has compiled specially for the students of B.A. sixth semester, Political science (major) under Dibrugarh University. It deals with women's issues, concepts, and women movements both in India and Europe and basis of women oppression. We hope that this book will be a book for all and not for the students or women only. We also hope that the present compilation will be found useful by all those who are interested to know the condition of women and the responsible factors of women oppression. We welcome readers' comments and suggestions on any aspect of this book. We too welcome constructive criticisms from the teachers and students for the improvement of this book. We acknowledge all those people who directly or indirectly help us to complete this task. We also acknowledge the contribution of our respective families whose support and encouragement has been a source of inspiration for us.

March 2014

Deepan Das
Tanusree Sarker
Rakhimoni Gogoi

SYLLABUS

Dibrugarh University
TDC (Major) 6th Semester
Paper: PSCM-602 (Introduction to Women's Studies)
Total Marks: 100
End Semester: 80 and Internal Assessment: 20

Objectives

The course is designed to generate sensitization for women's issues and problems. It will try to introduce the basic concepts and theories to facilitate the understanding of women's studies. The course will also try to introduce the students to women's activism in India and the West.

Unit I

Women's Studies—its meaning, nature, scope and objectives; Development of Women's Studies as a discipline.

(Lectures: 10 Marks: 16)

Unit II

Approaches to the study of Women's Studies—Liberal, Marxist, Radical and Third World. (Lectures: 10 Marks: 16)

Unit III

Basic concepts in Women's Studies—Patriarchy, Gender, Socialisation, Public-Private divide, Sexual division of labour.

(Lectures: 10 Marks: 16)

Unit IV

Women's Movements—Western and Indian—Origin, Growth, Issues and Present Status. (Lectures: 10 Marks: 16)

Unit V

Feminist analysis of Socio-cultural and institutional basis of Women's oppression—Family, Education, Economy, Religion, State and Media.

(Lectures: 10 Marks: 16)

Contents

Unit I
Understanding of Women's Studies

Introduction: Women studies mainly deal with women. It is a new subject developed only during 19th century. The subject got its importance when scholars starting to see women's need, functions and role from different perspectives. But the Women's Movement was really kicked off when first Women's Conference was held in Seneca Falls in America in 1848. It started to evaluate their role in both home and outside and fell the need for their own organisation.

Women's studies owe its existence to the movement for the liberation of women, the feminist movement exists because women are oppressed. Women's Studies diverse as its components are, has its Mission of a world free from sexism which includes commitments to free from all kind of national chauvinism free from all kinds of known, unknown bias targeted by society and by social norms. The development of women's studies at present time is the result of struggle to evolve knowledge, theory pedagogy and organizational models appropriate to that vision.

The Usefulness of women's studies has been its refusal to accept sterile division between academy and community, between growth of mind and the health of the body, between intellect and passion, between individual and society. It is indeed a way away from deconstruction of human being into different categories such as ethnic, racial, religious, economic, age and sexual orientation—which interact to produce complex dominating behaviour from one group to other groups.

Meaning of Women's Studies

Actually advocacy to bring about greater recognition for women's contribution in all aspects of society served as basis for women's studies. It is an endeavour suitable for concentrated study, arose from a grassroots movement of women's scholars and community activist who felt women's lives and perspectives were absent from the halls and clan rooms of advanced learning. As the public and private sphere of life started to depict more prominently the criticism about inequality and deprivation of women becoming more common. The new questions started to come up about gender discrimination, condition of working women, women's participation in freedom movement, their condition during war and peace time, sexual division of labour etc. Women's studies started to introduce this question. Women's Studies Draws special attention to the issues, like poverty, women in marginalized section, socio-economic condition of women, women's role in policy making etc.

Thus first concrete shape of women's studies as an academic discipline comes into existence only during 1970s when San Diego State College first initiated the study. It was during 1970s San Diego State College of USA where as an academic discipline, the Women's Studies came into existence.

Since its evolving as a subject matter "Women's Studies" owes its origin to "Feminist Movement". The word "feminism" comes from the Latin word "Femina" which mean women. It was **Mary Wollstonecraft's** "Vindication of the Rights of Women" (1792) which inspired feminist movement to evolve.

According to *Macmillan Dictionary*, Women's Studies means "to study the position and treatment of women in society".

Women's Studies are a multidisciplinary study of the social status and societal contribution of women and the relationship between power and gender.

Women's Studies also known as feminist studies are an interdisciplinary academic field that explores politics, society and history from women and/or feminist perspectives.

Nature of Women's Studies

Women's studies is inter-disciplinary in nature. Women's Studies programmes draw its much inspirations from practical field. It embedded theory with practical aspect of life. It focused on the power structures, oppression, inequality and social suffering. As it draws inspiration from feminist movement. Whereas the Sex-Gender dichotomy is becoming a controversial issue in Women's Studies. The feminism which attempts to demolish the whole fabric and all ideas which justify male superiority. Women's Study is the platforms for that Feminism the advocacy of women's right of which Women's Studies in the mirror. The public personal debate is very much genuine in Women's Studies. Women's Studies integrated academy with community, theoretical perspective with practical accomplishment. Women's Studies is a part of society and unlike other academic platform women's studies have drawn every inspiration from society, from practicality of women's life. It is, therefore, natural that every theory of women's studies have been influenced by the sufferings, subjugation of women. That is why, it refused to draw distinction in its study between individual and society, between academy and community. The integrating nature of mind body is always seen is Women's Studies.

Women's Studies as an academic discipline developed only during 1970s. Although 'Plato' can be known as the first feminist of the world for his justification of women's role in Politics and Society, but the true nature of feminist movement can be traced back to 19th century Seneca Conference. Women's Studies as a discipline got inspiration from feminist movement, suffragette movement (the Political Rights Movement), suppression that women experienced in every walk of life. It is a holistic approach towards empowering women.

Women's Studies is universal is nature. It studied universal problem that women faced like political rights, gender discrimination, discrimination in work place, social justices, health, education etc.

Women's Studies many times termed parallel with gender studies as both the two focuses on Gender and identity and multidisciplinary in nature. However, there are some fundamental differences between the two.

(a) Women's Studies analyze gender by focusing on women whereas Gender Studies may or may not focus on women.
(b) Women's Studies very much related with feminist movement, study, methodology which is not found in Gender Studies.
(c) Women's study emphasized only on women its both from theoretical and practical perspective but Gender Study emphasized both male and female.

Women's Study is an interdisciplinary academic field: Women's Studies is closely related to sociology, politics, economics, history, education, anthropology, literature, environment etc. Women's Studies discuss every aspect of social science independently. Moreover, the nature of Women's Studies is to analyse the projection of women by different fields of social science.

Women's Study is against patriarchy: Women's Studies identify patriarchy as the root cause of all sorts of oppression against women. It criticizes the exploitation, discrimination and torture against women in the patriarchal system and it wants to abolish patriarchal system to bring equality and justice for all in the society.

Women's Studies are related to the feminist thoughts: Women's Studies examine and analyse various issues and problems faced by women in different parts of the world. It also analyse the status of women, their rights and freedoms, their struggle against male domination. This study focuses on the emancipation of women, women education and social consciousness and improvement of their standard of living as well as their status in both social and political fields.

Another nature of women's study is it wants to create a new identity for women. In its study, the presence of women can feel in every aspect of society whether it is history, economies, science or environment. Women's Studies depicted how women is very much part of all. Its eco-feminism shows women's role in protecting environment.

Women's Studies encompass the deconstruction of traditional disciplines in terms of their subject matter and their structure. Women's Studies attempted to produce theories and concepts keeping in mind the feminist concerns and principles.

Objectives

The objectives of Women's Studies include—

1. Findings about women by raising new questions and accepting Women's perceptions and experiences as real and significant.
2. Correcting misconception about women and identifying ways in which traditional methodologies may distort knowledge.
3. Theorizing about the place of women's in society and appropriate strategies for change.
4. Examining the diversity of Women's experience and the ways which clan, race, sexual orientation and other variables intersect with gender.
5. Highlighting the social problems of women.
6. Academic analysis of the feminist thoughts.

Scope of Women's Studies

Women's Study is an interdisciplinary study. The scope of Women's Study is very vast ranging from Women's Movement and Politics to Women's Reproductive Behaviours, Leadership, Health and Religion. It broadening the concept of research and opened vistas in research like women as a subject in conflict. In Military Study, Defense Study and History they took Women for research. The Women's Studies also helped government in formulating policies. It will help the NGOs and other grassroots level organisations with their working and to plan the programme according to the needs of the women. As Women's Studies is a conglomeration academic and practical activity it can help to study the deprivation of women, their socio-economic status, their role as a marginalized section and bring out the truth. As developed due to result of Women's Movement, Women's Studies has their scope both in Social and Physical Science. In Social Sciences from Research to Policy formulation everywhere the need to study Women's condition become mandatory. But in Physical Sciences Scholars like Vandana Shiva played an important role in bringing up topic like ecofeminism through her book "**Staying Alive**". Women's Studies disseminate knowledge and field action. Women's Studies now being an independent teaching department its development gave mid-range of ideas to accumulate. As Research is a part of it, interdisciplinary research including de-construction and reconstruction of theories, developing of new ideas will help the students to get a broad knowledge of it.

As it has broad vistas Women's Study can be seen in wider content of common democratic struggles, of linking women's rights to the rights of other marginalized groups. Women's Studies have its scope among the media study also. Film and other media which played important role in society. And have greatest impact on it can be studied through Women's Studies.

Women and their issues are basically the subject matter of Women's Studies. These discipline studies women comprehensively—their lives, struggles, works, desires, accomplishments and every other things related to their lives. It studies the status of women in society, and their contribution to its progress. It also studies the role of women in different aspects as economic, political, legal or moral.

Human rights which are inherent for every human being many time violated in case of women and children. Women's Study can take up those issues too.

Development of Women's Studies an Academic Discipline

Development of Women's Studies can be traced back to the Feminist Movement that has been carried out by scholars, like Marry Wollstonecraft, *A Vindication of Rights of Women* (1792), J.S. Mill, *The Subjection of Women* (1869). Jean de Meung, Marie de Gurney. The Feminist Movement first began out of reform groups such as the Abolition of Slavery, Social Purity and Tempera Movement. Women started to realize this position in the society and started campaign on issue ranging from guardianship of infants, property rights, divorce, access to higher education, equal pay and safety of the female workers. The period between 1790-

1860 may be called the beginning of the Feminist Movement dominated by the enlightenment ideas. **Margarett Fuller, Elizabeth Starton**, Lucretia Mott were some of the early activists of the Movement.

Increasingly as women started to feel the need for their political rights. Feminist started campaign for Women's Suffrage separate from and independent of political parties and other organised groups. As a result, in 1928, Women got to cast their first ever right to vote in Britain. It was known as Suffrage Movement (1860-1930).

During 1940s and 1950s women took up challenges and started doing jobs ranging from White Collar Jobs to Labour Trade Union Workers.

The Second Wave Feminism grew in the shadow of movements launched by students and blacks in 1960s. This shows radicalization of the Feminist Movement. "Women's Liberation" became the top most priority. The Private Public demand crop up. And right to abortion on demand, free childcare provision and equal pay came up. It was during the Second academe wave feminism that Women's Studies as a discipline first emerged. This condition of the academic world to a Social Movement meant that the setting up and teaching of such courses was a profoundly political act. It is connected to social change which was broadly defined the recognition and analysis of women's oppression, and therefore, how to this subordination in patriarchal and capitalist societies.

Although debates always there whether feminist Movement is responsible for development of Women's Studies. However, it needs to be admitted that feminist ideas like personal being political, separation between Public and Private sphere, Oppression that women faced due to her gender, sin, clan, caste, ethnicity and age were some of the important developments which influenced Women's Studies.

As an academic discipline the Women's Studies was modelled as American Studies and Ethnic Studies. The first two W.S.P. in the US were established in 1970 at San Diego State College and Sunny—BUFFALO. Both the Colleges before taking up the projects made intensive programme on organizing rallies, getting views of the people especially women, operating unofficial classes etc. Carol Rowell Council was the student co-founder along with Dr. Joyce Knower. SUNY BUFFALO programme was also the result of intense debate on feminist perspective led by Elizabeth Kennedy and it was birthed out of the American Studies departments. In 1972, Sarah Lawrence College became the first institution to grant Master's degree in Women's History.

In Britain, women involved with left politics and the Women's Movement in the 1960s and 1970s began to set up Women's Studies Courses within higher education and in an adult education content, and it was in the latter where, for instance, Women's health, history and self-assertiveness courses developed. As the constraints of formal assessment and required qualification which characterized higher education need not apply to Women's Studies it allowed Women more control over educational prices.

Though, there are some courses offered in Britain within Polytechniques and Universities, but it was only in 1980 that the first M.A. was offered in Women's Studies, at the University of Kent. Gradually, Post Graduate Courses followed by Under Graduate Courses. On the other hand, in India, the first University research centre for Women's Studies was set up in 1974 by the SNDT Women's University, Mumbai. The University Grants Commission has played a significant role in developing Women's Studies as a discipline in India.

Despite various criticisms Women's Studies began to develop in various College and Universities in Europe, North-America, and South America, Asia and Africa. It started to offer varying degree of courses and have begun to conceptualize in various approach.

MODEL QUESTIONS

A. Very Short Type Questions (1 Mark for Each)

1. Who is regarded as the first feminist of the World?
2. Name the author of the book "Subjection of Women"?
3. Who wrote the book "Vindication of Women's Right"?
4. What do you mean by "Suffrage Movement"?
5. Mention the period known as "First Wave Feminist Movement"?

6. Who is known as the pioneer of Women's Studies in India?
7. Who wrote the book "Le Deuscieme Sexes"?
8. Name the author of the book "A Room of Ones Own".
9. When for the first time, the term "Feminism" was used?
10. Name the College where Women's Studies were started?
11. Who is the pioneer of Women's Studies in India?
12. Which decade was declared as "International Women's decade"?
13. Who wrote the book "The Second Sex"?

B. Short Type Questions (4/5 Marks for Each)

1. Distinguish between Women's Studies and Gender Studies.
2. Nature of Women's Studies.
3. Objectives of Women's Studies.
4. Define Women's Studies.
5. Impediments of Women's Participation in Politics.
6. Importance of Women's Studies.

C. Easy Type Questions (10/12 marks each)

1. Define Women's Studies. Discuss its Nature and Scope.
2. Discuss about the evolution of Women's Studies as an Academic Discipline.
3. Define Women Studies. Distinguish between Women Studies and Gender Studies.
4. Examine the relation between Women Studies and Economics and History.
5. What do you mean by Women's Studies? Discuss its theoretical roots.
6. Discuss Women's Studies as a discipline of study.
7. What are the challenges to Women's Studies? Discuss its development as an academic discipline.
8. Discuss the significance of Women Studies as a academic discipline.
9. Define Women's Studies. Discuss its importance.

Unit II
Approaches to the Study of Women's Studies

Introduction: The women studies have approaches based on which many ideas are born out. The Women's Studies itself is such a critical thing that summing it up under one or two approach is very difficult. However, for the betterment of the study the Women's Studies are divided into following categories—

(a) Liberal Approach
(b) Marxist Approach
(c) Radical Approach
(d) Third World Approach.

Liberal Approach to the Study of Women's Studies

The word "Liberalism" comes from the Latin word 'Liber' which means 'freedom'. The Liberal feminist's main idea is to attain freedom from all kinds of suppression. The Liberal feminist desire absolute freedom and equal rights with men. During 18th century, Mary Wollstonecraft in her book "A Vindication of the Rights of Women" tried to highlight the right to education for women. That education for women is very essential. This was the very first step towards liberal feminist ideas. Liberal feminism got its momentum when J.S. Mill put forward his theory on liberalism. Moreover, Betty Friedan, Gloria Steinam, Naomi Wolf etc. popularized the idea.

Evolution of Liberal Feminist Ideas: J.S. Mill put forward his ideas on Liberalism in the book "**On Liberty**" and later on his another famous book "**Principles of Political Economy**". In both the books, he talked about compulsory education for all, equal wages, introduction of Factory Laws, Public Health, Old Age Pension, Equality etc. Based on that many liberalists put forward their ideas. The Liberal Feminist also took some noticeable steps based on that. However, Marry Wollstonecraft put forward her ideas about liberalism much earlier in the year 1792. With her book "Vindication on the Rights of Women". But, Liberal Feminist in its true sense starts with the First Wave of Feminism. In this First Wave Feminism Elizabeth Caddy Stanton (1815-1900) became instrumental in Seneca Falls, New York. Stanton supported Women Suffrage Movement, and liberalist ideas on Divorce, Custody rights, Employment and Income rights etc. One of the most successful leaps of the liberal feminist idea was passing of the bill "Married Women's Property Act, 1848 by New York State of U.S.A. However, it was on August 26, 1920, that the 19th Amendment to the U.S. Constitution becomes Law and Women got right to Suffrage.

After the Second World War the objectives of the Liberal Feminist started to change. During 1960s and 70s the feminist focus in the United States was on women as individual and the narrower of their lives. Betty Freidan's famous book "**The feminine Mystique**" claimed that women's role as a good mother and wife considered more respectable rather than a successful working Women. Freidan's book which was published in the year 1963 leads to the beginning of Second Wave Feminism. She criticized the attitude of women and how they were misled in their role as mother, wife by advertising company, by patriarchal society. She also found it those Women of America who earlier during fifties were very much Career Oriented and wanted to build a niche for their own now becoming more inclined towards Marriage and Motherhood. But the study that drew attention of the World was because of its finding that Women are not very much happy in their life although they have everything that they wanted. The Women very much tried to idealize the '**Happy House Wife**' image projected by the Media at that time. It leads to publishing of many articles alleging and counter alleging Freidan's Article. This became the starting point of Second Wave Feminism and also liberal feminism. Liberal feminist started to criticise the role of various agencies for projecting Women in downgrading way. Women are not object are showpiece but they need equal treatment in the hands of Government and from others. The Liberal Feminist believe that there is no difference between Male and Female and as everyone is individual human being so equal treatment should be given to all. Women should have some legal rights as man. They wanted to eliminate discrimination against Women. This goal of feminism was termed as "Undoing Gender", Politically Liberal feminists focus has been on visible sources of Gender discrimination, such as Gender Job Markets and inequitable Wage Scales. The Liberal Feminist has developed theories to explain gendered segregation of jobs. Here generally men work with men and Women with Women. This will lead to Gender Stratification of Organizational Hierarchies (in most cases, the top of business always belong to the men). Liberal Feminist wanted to eliminate that stratification. They believe that division of labour should be on the basis of expertisement on the subject rather than on gender. More over, during 1970s and 1980s, Liberal Feminist supported reproduction right and accent to abortion. According to them, Giving birth to a child is not a women's go end make end or ultimatum in life. She has every other right just like any other men living in her vicinity. The Liberal Feminist with the passage of time started to demand justice on sexual harassment, Voting, education, fair compensation for work, affordable, childcare, Healthcare and highlight the intensity of growing domestic violence issue and sexual violence issue among women.

Some of the Popular Liberal Feminist Thinkers

(a) *18th century thinkers:* Mary Wollstonecraft, Harriet Jubman.
(b) *19th century thinkers:* John Stuart Mill, Harriet Tailor, Eleanor Roosevelt, Elizabeth Stanton.
(c) *20th century thinkers:* Betty Friedon, Gloria Steinem, Rebecca Walker, Naomi Wolf, Hillary Clinton.

Some of the famous Feminist Organizations are—The National Organization for Women (NOW), The National Women

Political Caucus, The Women's Equality Action League, Feminist Majority Foundation and Ms. Magazine.

The main features or attributes of Liberal Feminist Theory are:

(a) Liberal feminist believe that personal rights should predominate over concerns for the social good. The Liberal Feminist believes on individual rights over group or social rights.

(b) Although, the idea of Liberal Feminist was tossed during 18th century but it became popular only during first half of 20th century.

(c) Liberal feminist seek equal rights of with men and believe that individual should be treated not on the basis of sex, money or inheritance, but they should be treated in accordance with their talents and effort and for their equality.

(d) They campaign to remove any obstacle, be it Political, Social, Legal or Economical that gets in the way of women having the same opportunities as their Male counterparts.

(e) Liberal feminist approach successfully eradicate certain laws which discriminate Men and Women.

(f) Liberal feminist theory was mainly popular in us and from their it extended to the whole world.

(g) Liberal feminism claims that Gender differences are not based on biology and therefore, women and men are not different.

(h) Liberal feminism is responsible for popularizing the ideology of "Gender Mainstreaming".

(i) Liberal feminism tried to eradicate Sexual Division of Labour.

Criticism of the Liberal Approach to the Study of Women's Studies

1. Liberal feminist ideas many times contradict with their own view.
2. Liberal feminist views of be Gendered society is not possible. 'Womanliness' is a very unique character of Women. Child birth, Nurturance, Empathy, Care,

Pregnancy is something which Women can possess. Liberalist believes that this can make a Women's role bit lower is only a misconception.

3. Personal rights and enjoyment of Personal liberty cannot bring development in the Society. Society can be progressed only when overall development happen. It can be possible only when as a ground society is progressed.

Marxist Approach to the Study of Women's Studies

Marxist feminism arises out of the doctrine of Karl Marx, whose theory generally evolved/talked about rights of the oppressed class people. His theory of Class Struggle highlighted the fact that oppressor and oppressed people stood in constant opposition to one another. Marxism denounced subjugation of Women in an era or in the century when people still supported subjugation of Women. Marxism strongly advocated that women's oppression is not a permanent feature in history but the result of a certain social formation and that the relationship between the Sexes are not natural but socially constructed. Marx and Engel both believed that when workless or oppressed class will realise that they are being exploited in the hands of Bourgeoisie then they will start revolt against Capitalist. And ultimately Classless society will be established. Marxists are opposed to any kind of enslavement including enslavement of women. From its inception, Marxists Movement has championed female equality and Women's rights Marxism believed that Women's Oppression cannot be eradicated in a day. It can be eliminated only when it overturned the Capitalist System. Moreover, Marxist ideas believe that Women serves as the material interest of the ruling class. Women by giving birth to children generally produce next generation at low cost. Also, women can be more likely to be engaged in low paid job than Men. Women become useful during economic crisis or during lean economic period.

Friedrich Engel in his book "*The Origin of the Family, Private Property and the State*" (1884) analyzed Gender oppression and argues that a women's subordination is not a result of biological frame but it is society and male domination which subjugated her rights. The female oppression is the deeply rooted form of oppression in the society which is created by the society and to eradicate it will take a long time. Friedrich also observed that in the Primitive Society when people were dependent on hunting and fishing for their livelihood the Women at that time was not regarded as the Second Class Citizen. However, as the time passes people started to possess Movable and Immovable Property. The idea of notes and currencies, trades etc. started to began. This economic determinant changes the social strata. In many areas, it is class which started to divide the society. With all this, Women's position is slowly started to sink and later on, Women are regarded as Second Class Citizen. The capitalist regarded as the 'Reserve Army of Labour'. Rosa Luxemburg in the year 1972 commented on rich women as 'docile lamb' in the camps of Conservative and Religion Clerics.

According to Marxist feminism, it is the law of inheritance which made the male domination over women in case of Property, thus making the situation difficult for women. In patriarchal, civilization Women have been subjected to a specific kind of repression and their mental and physical development has been channelled in a specific direction. This subjugation leads to Feminist Movement. The link between Feminist Movement and Marxism is that both wanted oppressed to be free.

Marxist feminist fried to identify the operation of Gender relation. It tried to explore the relations amongst the organization of Sexuality, domestic production, the household and so on, and historical change in the mode of production, system of appropriation and exploitation. Marxist feminists have argued that Marxism must need to take into account exploitation that women faced in the hands of powerful class. Parxism needs to take into account problem of Women's poor wage, domestic labour and how the patriarchal influence exploited them throughout their life. Marxist Feminist based their argument on the corruption of wage labour which itself is a class distinction. According, to Marx, Wage Labour is a form of 'Exploitation' and 'Prostitution' of Labour.

The Basic Principle of Marxian Approach to the Study of Women's Studies

(a) Capitalist class relationships are the root cause behind female oppression, exploitation and discrimination;

(b) Patriarchy is a result of economic exploitation of people;
(c) The family system is nothing but reproduction of Labour Power;
(d) Capitalist considered Women as reserved Labour Power;
(e) According to Marxist Feminist Theory Women played the role of 'Domestic Servant' for man as they played the role of Wife, Sister or Mother.
(f) The main ambition of Marxism is to overthrow Capitalism. In this connection, they included Women within greater periphery of Oppressed Class.
(g) For Marxist Feminist theory Social relations of production (where Women played major role), forces of production (Sexual division of labour), Man of Production (owned by Men) in the economic base of which ideologies of Gender and Social institutions are paid to be Superstructure.
(h) For Marxist Feminists, the concept of Social class is considered to be more important than the concept of Patriarchy as patriarchy is nothing but the result of class exploitation.
(i) Marxist Feminist believed that the Women played dual role of both child reared and Worker in the Modern Society. Men are able to exploit this dual service of women within the home.

Marxist feminist is mostly based on "Base and Superstructure" Model. According to this theory Gender distinction is economic rather than anatomical. The Force of Production is so strong that since Primitive time men owned means of production whereas Women played only Second fiddle. Moreover, Sexual division of labour originated from the economic means of production.

Criticism of the Marxian Approach to the Study of Women's Studies

1. Marxist view of women as child reared and unpaid worker is totally wrong. Women played the role of mother, wife, sister or daughter not by force but by their own will. It is natural and society formed only when this role will not be categorized on economic basis.

2. Marxist feminist theory ignores family which is base for any developmental society.
3. The rate of exploitation depends on the value of Power. The value of Power equals value of commodities necessary for its production. Marxian theory, however, ignored this all things.
4. According to Liberal Feminist Theorist, the Marxist feminist theorists view that the gender in equality is very much common in capitalist society only. However, according to Liberalist, in Socialist Communist Country also gender inequality is very much visible.
5. Marxist feminist views on gender inequality can be reduced by various reforms which is now-a-days seen among capitalist country.
6. Although Marxist feminist talked about Capitalist and Patriarchy but they paid least attention to it.

Marxist feminist ideas which developed during 19th century got its momentum only during 1970s when the United State's Government passed the Equal Pay Act, 1970. The Equal Pay or Equal Wages to workers irrespective of gender is one of the highlight of present day Gender equality.

Radical Approach to the Study of Women's Studies

The Radical Feminist ideas started to develop during 1960s when the Second wave feminist started to develop. The emergence of 'Women's right', to perceiving the nation that 'Personal is Political' defined the Liberal Movement which turned into radical during the later period of 1960s. The first 'Radical Feminist Organisation' was found by women like Shulamith Firestone; Jo Freeman in the year 1967. This organisation was known as "Radical Women". These two women who were earlier member of new left and Liberal Movement felt that a women's organisation is needed to fulfil the demand of the women. This led them to develop as organisation only for women. They included the word "radical" in order to describe their stand for Women's rights. The radical feminist comes into limelight by criticizing liberal feminist ideas. The Civil Right Movement in the year 1967 a group of New York Women allied with Ti-Grace Atkinsan an early feminist organisation known as ..."The October 17th Movement" which later known as the "Feminist". This was the first of its kind radical feminist organisation.

According to Kathie Sarachild, the word "radical" means roots. And the feminist theorists are interested into getting to the roots of the problem.

Radical feminist beliefs that women's oppression is the most fundamental form of oppression. The key concept of the Radical feminist is Patriarchy. All societies are seen operating against the interests of women in favour of interests of men. Patriarchy is seen as important source of women's exploitation than capitalism. Radical Feminist Movement started with the start of second Wave Feminist Movement. The Radical Feminists challenge the social norms and customs of the society as it has Patriarchal element all over.

Evolution of Radical Feminism

Basically start up in United States of America (USA) the idea of "Radical Feminism", however, imparted to United Kingdom by its Scholars. In the Year 1967, the first Radical Feminist Organisation was born. Its name was "Radical Women" (USA). Later on it become more popular in U.K. But due to lack of co-ordination among the radical feminist of U.K. in 1970s it divided into two groups—Socialist and Radical. Again another group emerged known as "Revolutionary Feminist".

Moreover, a new awareness among the Women and the Scholars of World started to develop. Radical feminist thrives for equality and criticize that Patriarchy is the primary source of exploitation over women rather than individual man. The radicalists in the year 1968 protested against in America beauty pageant. It was said to be the earliest conscious movement in America among Women. Many women in order to protest against male domination thrown their high hauls, beauty bon and "other instrument of female torture". They believe these as a symbol of oppression. The radical feminist later on of Kate Millet's "**Sexual Politics**" (1969) deals with the oppression of Women in a variety of sociological and ideological constructs. Later on, Dale Spender's "**Man Made Language**" (1980) proved this point forcefully in respect of gender bias in language. With the debacle of Russia and with the advent of new technology, the Women's Movement gained a new direction. The primary demands of the Women like equal pay, equal political rights, and right to education are getting fulfilled. However, till now, we could not eradicate many of problems faced by women like sexual harassment, dowry, human (girl) trafficking, exploitation in jobs etc.

Radical feminist theory challenges not merely the imperfect realization of equal rights but the root concepts of individualism, rational deliberation and freedom through autonomy that underlies "Liberal Legalism".

The 19th century amendment which was passed in 1920 was seen as a turning point in separating Liberal feminism with Radical feminism. It was because the radicalists believed that women were historically the first oppressed group and most widespread. It exists in every where. It views sexual inequality as a systematic and deliberative victimization of women by a socially constructed Male hierarchy that is reinforced by Liberal law. Radicalists believed that social rules deprive women of equality. The sexual inequality created lots of suffering among women. Therefore, it tried to eliminate the sex/gender as a concept of class system.

Catherine Mackinon of "Towards a feminist theory" believes that male domination over women is due to physiological nature. Radicalist Movement truly believes on that idea. Ary Allen puts it as "Radical" feminist tends to understand power in terms of dyadic relations of dominance/subordination, often understood or analogy with the relationship between Master and Slave.

The radical feminism can be divided into two forms—(a) Radical Liberation and (b) Radical Cultural Feminist.

The radical libertarian beliefs comes from the idea that gender is an aspect that in separate from sex, and that male dominated societies place unyielding gender rules to control Women. The radical liberalism believed in freedom of women in every sense. They oppressed family notion or idea of family, Motherhood, free hand to choose their partners etc. They wanted to defy the norms of society and wanted to be free from the bondage of Patriarchy.

The Radical Cultural Feminist opposes the on going social norms and customs of the society. Radical Cultural Feminist opposed all kinds of those materials which makes women subordinate Second Class Citizen. According to Radical Cultural Feminist Women are natural mothers. They wanted rights over female reproduction. They wanted gender sensitization of men. The concepts like legalization of abortion, contraceptive pills, In-Vitro Fertilization (IVF) are some of the controversial things supported by Radical Cultural Group.

Basic Principles of Radical Feminism

(a) The concepts of Patriarchy and Sex class are key ideas in relation to the understanding of Women's position and experience in all societies.

(b) Radical feminism believes that Patriarchy has existed in all human societies.

(c) Patriarchal relationship is considered to be the way for capitalist form of economic and gender exploitation.

(d) Sexual inequality is institutionalised in society. It is not possible to achieve sexual equality through legal means are by changing people's attitude.

(e) Men are the enemy of women. Women are a sex class as they share a common interest in freeing themselves from Male oppression.

(f) The Universal causes of Patriarchy are considered to be—

  (i) The exploitation of females biology by men (e.g. Pregnancy).

  (ii) Marriage based family relationship in which men control women's behaviour.

  (iii) Heterosexual relations.

(g) One solution to the problem of Patriarchal exploitation is seen to be lesbian relationship and female support groups.

(h) Some Radical Feminists, like Firestone, argue that female emancipation can be achieved technologically (Women being freed from childbirth etc.).

(i) In general Radical Feminist sees the exploitation of women as involving both the Public sphere and Private sphere.

However, this dual form of exploitation is not usually experienced by men.

State and Society are oppressive institution which perpetuates patriarchy.

Criticism of Radical Feminist Approach

(i) Radical feminist theory of Patriarchy is said to be descriptive rather than analytical in nature. It enables to explain the origin of male power and therefore, unable to provide an adequate strategy for ending it.
(ii) Some believes that it is based on wrong notion of "Men as the enemy".
(iii) The theory is said to be a historical and based on a false universalism that reflects only the experiences of White Middle Class women and obscure the very different problem faced by Working class, Black and Third World Women.
(iv) Radical feminist made the Women passive victim rather than the Co-makers of history and the agents of change in the future.
(v) There is no real evidence that women constitute a "sex class".
(vi) The radical feminist defy the Pure and Sacred Custom of Marriage, which is a binding force in any Social System.
(vii) Giving importance to Radical Feminism means breakdown of Social system.

The Socialist Feminist never believe women as "sex class" nor do they see all men as "the Class enemy". Moreover, not all male-female relationship is based on oppression and exploitation.

The Radical Feminist theory tries to expose domination both at public and private sphere. There are various writers who gave views regarding the growth and development of Feminist Theory. But, the ultimate ideas are that Radical feminism helped to build up a World where Women can give their views without fear.

Third World Feminist Approach

Third World Feminism is a form of feminist philosophy which centres on the idea like Racism, Colonialism, Sexual Division of Labour, Political dominance etc. The Post Colonial Feminism is the feminist idea which is developed on Colonial nations. These theorists believed that Third World Feminist rise by criticizing the Radical Western Philosophy. Gayatri Chakravorty Spivak explains that the term "Third World" was initially coined in the years 1955 by those emerging from the Old World Order. The initial attempt in the Bandung Conference (1955) was to establish a third way—neither with the Eastern nor within the Western block—in the World system in response to the emerging New World Order established after the Second World War was not accompanied by a commensurate intellectual effort. According to Kumkum Sagary "Third World is a term that both signifies and blurs the functioning of an economic, political and imaginary geography that able to unite vast and vastly differentiated areas of the world into a Single Underdeveloped Terrain. The Third World Feminism very famously dealt with the problem faced by the Women of Underdeveloped Third World Countries. The Western Feminist very much spread out the idea of feminism towards the World. The problems of the Third World Women was not portrayed in a serious way. Moreover, the Western Feminist ignored the voices of Non-White, Non-Western Women for many years. Thus creating resentment from feminist in developing nations is the problem that Post-colonial Women faced in the Third World country is something which is not faced by first World Civilization. The problems like Communalism, Dowry, *Sati*, Migration, Sexual division of labour, suppression etc. Women are regarded as Second Class citizen in some areas of India. The Foetus Determination and Honour Killing, Dowry, Sati are some of the customs that made women a degraded soul. Third World feminism is also described as Post-Colonial feminism. In Post-Colonial World, feminist begins its journey by challenging Women's role in both home front and outside home. She negotiates her obstacles in that home front like Dowry, Honour Killing, Rape etc. and also has to juggle between Home and Work place. Post-Colonial feminism is an exploration of and at the intersections of Colonialism and Neo-colonialism and Neo-colonialism with Gender, Nation, Class, Race and Sexualities in different contexts of Women's lives, their work, sexuality and rights.

Post-Colonial or Third World Feminism tried to bring out the problems faced by the women of a Third World country. The Third World Feminism found similarity between decolonized or just independent nations and women within Patriarchal System.

Features of Third World Feminism

The Basic features of Third World Feminism are as follows—

1. It stressed more on basic needs of women.
2. Third World feminism wanted equal stand not only in case of Gender but also equality in case of race, class and nations asymmetries.
3. They criticize Western feminism and believe that basic goals of Western Feminism and Third World Feminism are very different.
4. The Third World Feminist Scholars are mostly from Third World Countries who understand the situation of Women in Third World in a better way.
5. The issues pertaining to Third World Feminism is very basic like Welfare of Women, Eradication of Poverty, Banned on Sati, Dowry, Fetus Killing etc.
6. The Third World Feminism basically developed during 1980s and 1990s.
7. They believed in equal existence.
8. The Western Feminism opt for Sexual Liberation whereas Third Word Feminist support freedom from sexualisation etc.

Criticism

(a) The Third World Feminist theory is supported by a very few scholars, it is yet to get momentum.

(b) Third World Feminism believes in overall protection of identity, but even after so many years the Women still becoming victim of discrimination and violence.

(c) Third World Feminism is very much against Western Model of Feminism.

MODEL QUESTIONS

A. Very Objectives Type Questions (1 Mark Each)

1. Who wrote the book "The Dialectic of Sex"?
2. Name the author of the book "Sexual Politics"?
3. ——authored the book "The Second Sex".
4. One Proponent of Radical feminism?
5. What do you mean by "Approach"?
6. Name the Proponent of Marxist Approach to the study of Women's Studies.
7. What do you mean by "Second Wave of Feminism"?
8. Who wrote the book "The Feminine Mystique"?
9. Mention any two advocate of Liberal Approach to Women's Studies.
10. When "Married Women's Property Act" was passed?
11. Who wrote the book "The Origin of the Family, Private Property and the State"?
12. "Wage Labour is a form of Exploitation and Prostitution of Labour"—who said?

(B) Short Type Questions (4/5 Marks Each)

1. Basic assumption of Liberal Approach to Women's Studies.
2. Characteristic of Liberal Approach to Women's Studies.
3. Criticism of Liberal Approach to Women's Studies.
4. Basic features of Marxist Feminism.
5. Criticism of Marxist approach to Women's Studies.
6. Views of Simon de Beauvoir on Radical Feminism.
7. Views of Kate Millet's on Radical Feminism.

(C) Long Type Questions (10/12 Marks)

1. Discuss about the Liberal Approach to the study of Women's Studies.

2. Critically analyse the Marxist Approach to the study of Women's Studies.
3. Discuss critically about Radical Approach to the study of Women's Studies.
4. Assess the Third World Approach to the study of Women's Studies.

Unit III
Basic Concepts in Women's Studies

Patriarchy

Patriarchy is one of the very powerful words. Patriarchy practices, colonizes and rules the Physical World. Patriarchy is not a term but a Psycho-social belief that runs into the blood of the human being since the time immemorial. It is one way of showing subordination of women to men. Patriarchal element in society leads to violation against women. It leads to discrimination, suppression and exploitation of women by men. Patriarchy according to Oxford Dictionary means a society, system or country that is ruled or controlled by men. In simple terms it means rule of the father in a male dominated family. It is a social and ideological construction of family which beliefs females to be more attractive. In Gender Politics, the term 'Patriarchy' refers to any form of social power given disproportionately to men. Patriarchy is based on a system of power relations which are hierarchical and unequal where Men control Women's Production, Reproduction and Sexuality. However, the nature and subjugations of women varies from Society to Society. Patriarchy in simple means Male Domination, Male Superiority.

The patriarch is usually an elderly Male person who has influence over others. Many Feminists consider patriarchy to be the basis on which most modern societies have been formed. A good number of feminists use the term 'Patriarchy' as a shorthand for male authority and male dominated society. It is necessary to get away from this model in order to achieve gender equality Due to Patriarchal concept in the society men need not have to fight for their rights whereas women always need to fight to have had their genuine rights. (Bhasis *op. cit.*, p. 5). The feminist writers since their inception in the early 20th century have been fighting against and has been criticizing Patriarchal element in the society. The critics always started their writing by criticizing Patriarchal element in the society which dominates the women members in the society. The Feminist Scholars have developed many theories to understand Patriarchy.

The two major ways in which Patriarchy controls people are with the built-in environment and mind control with the Mass Media. The Modern life style, Working Environment, Society contributes in developing Patriarchal element in the Society. Patriarchy deliberately takes a negative view of the human society, its nature and human nature. Moreover, as the World now becomes more developed, the suppression and exploitation of women become more and more prominent. The Patriarchal mindset wanted women to object. It is seen that religion played a very important role is creating patriarchal element is the society. The scriptures like Manusmriti, Bible, Quaran played important role in creating differences and ways of dominance for Women. Under Patriarchy, different kinds of evidence may be used to control and subjugate women and such evidences may even be considered legitimate. It is not uncommon in patriarchy to have some oppressed element playing important role in their own subjugation. Women without knowing participated for the benefits of male, e.g. Women models in various Male needed things, Women favouring male child over female, many times to retain their privileges women subjugated women.

The nature and control of subjugation of Women varies from one society to the other due to differences in Class, Caste, Religion, Region, Ethnicity and Socio-Cultural Concept. Thus, in India Brahminical Patriarchy; Tribal Patriarchy and Dalit Patriarchy are different from each other. Similarly, subordination of Women in developed countries is different from developing countries. The Traditionalists view Patriarchy as biologically determined. As biologically Men and Women are different so their functions also need to be differentiated.

Origins of Patriarchy

The origins of Patriarchy or the set of social and behavioural norms are closely related to the concept of Gender roles that are considered to be socially appropriate for individuals of a specific sex. Before the nineteenth century the idea was basically 'theological', however, the 'origin of species' from Darwin's changes the Notion. The term 'Patriarchy' comes from the Ancient Greek word "Patriarches" which means a society where power was held by and passed down through the elder Males.

The term 'Patriarchal society' consists of a Male dominated Power structure throughout organized society and an individual relationship in which a male member is considered to be head of the family. It establishes male dominance control over Women's productive power, their production and sexuality. According to Marxrist principle, in primitive societies as the main tools of livelihood were hunting and gathering so there was a very simple division of labour, but not domination of women.

However, with the emergence of the concept of 'Private Property' the domination of Men by Women started. Women's subordination is not the result of her biological but from social arrangement. *Gerda Lerner,* the famous feminist writer believes that the beginning of the process of patriarchy started during somewhere Second Millennium Before Christ (B.C.) and may be completed by 500-600 B.C. So, during that period the Process of Changes in the society with idea of the process of enslavement began. But, the Sexual differences were till then very Lazy. However, with the changing time during later bronze period, as System of Marriage slowly started to evolve with it enslavement of women. The Suppression of Women which started with agricultural system, becomes more prominent after women were recognized as property and object of reproduction. Friedrich Engel's famous book, **The Origins of the Family' Private Property and the State**. (New York: International Publishers, 1970) stated that Private Property is the creation of Patriarchal system in the society. (Weitz, Rose, 2003), **The Politics of Women's Bodies Sexuality, Appearance and Behaviour**, New York: Oxford University Press) traced back origin of Patriarchy. Even in the writings of Aristotle when Aristotle assumed that women is defective part of humanity. During the medieval century this idea becomes at its peak. Even in Hinduism we traced back origin of

Patriarchy to '*Manu Sanhita*'. The element 'Patriarchy' becomes more prominent during the time of Greeks and Romans and aftermath. In fact, after month of Jesus Christ and in later development process Suppression of Women became more and more. As the idea of kingdom and its spreading began. Women become victim of exploitation. During Medieval Century, Subjugation of Women become more and she was blamed for the first sin ever committed in the sanctuary of Eden.

With capitalist economy at its progress women started to become an object. They were used for the means of production as cheap labour. The 19th and first part of 20th century also made them object of enjoyment and cheap labour. Eventually, during that time with the writings of Engel, Wollstonecraft, Beavoir, the idea of feminism started to grow. But the Capitalist Industrialist Policies already made them vulnerable. Hundreds of years of exploitation stripped them of their legal rights. They become objects in the advertisements even if the product is meant for Male. Further more, the debate about Public and Private Sphere started to show. The Capitalist also leads to more and more Sexual division of Labour. Women in earlier days considered property of her master. She has no property rights. The ideas like Good Wife, Mother, Good Daughter compelled her to be at home doing domestic labour all the time to satisfy the Patriarchal ideas of Male members of the family. The idea of family is one of the very basic ideas of 'Patriarchy' where father or husband or son is the sole ruler of the home.

Now-a-days, however, we see that as ideas started to change with First, Second and Third Wave of Feminism may become more optimistic towards Women's Rights. Now, there is less 'Sexual division of labour' in writings. But practically till now women is seen everywhere, especially among the women. The words like Dowry, Rape, Sexual Exploitation at work place, less wages for women, are still a cause of concern. The various Governmental Policies although highlight equality and wanted to give a good start to the rights of Women. But, still debate on Public Private Sphere is there.

The origin of patriarchy can be analyzed from three different perspectives—firstly, Engel's Theory which believed that women's subjugation began with the development of Private Property. Secondly, Radical feminist believes that Patriarchal distinction is due to biological difference between man and women. Thirdly, we can sum up that not only Private Property and Biology or Physiology, but Patriarchy is the creation of amalgamation of all conditions of society which include ideology and religion.

Structures of Patriarchy

Walby defined six structures of Patriarchy and these are as follows—

1. Paid workers form first structures of patriarchy. The women paid workers got less payment for same amount of work led to the first structure.
2. The Gender division of labour in the household which forced women to take primary responsibility for domestic work, rearing of children etc.
3. Culture plays a very important role in defining patriarchy. We have seen that in maximum cases the subjugation of women is happened in the name of culture. Our Mythology plays determinant role in saving our culture. However, this culture itself made women an object of use. The Modern Western Culture emphasizes is more on degrading women through their various remarks and used women's feminine attractiveness.
4. Heterosexual relationships are seen as a Patriarchal element.
5. Male Violence against women both in 'home front and in offices seen as structures of Patriarchy.
6. State plays a very dominant and Patriarchal role in dividing Male and Female.

However there are some other elements which we cannot rule out while discussing Structures of Patriarchy. Gerda Lerner believes that family is the basic structure of Patriarchy. It is a hierarchical system which binds the society. Almost, in all cases man is considered the head of the family thus control women both physically and psychologically. She is the tool to produce male inheritor of the family. Thus, family becoming the first structure of Patriarchy. Even in Matrilineal society, man plays the dominant role in a very invisible way.

The Second Structure of Patriarchy can be educational institutions. A systematic way of subordinating women started with educational system, where for hundreds of years women were debarred from enlarging and having knowledge at educational institutions. Later, although now women are allowed but expiration of patriarchy was seen through depiction of women as pure women, sacrificing image of women, a very obedient wife, adoring daughter, mother etc.

Religion and Religious institutions are another patriarchal construction. Religion plays an important role of restricting women's role. Women were debarred from doing certain religious activities, domination of male superiority, restriction on women in some religious places, imposition of *purdah*. Heroic depiction of Male gods etc. all symbolise inferior status of women.

Inheritance of property is another very important dimension of Gender Structure. Here Male is the sole inheritor of property since the time idea of property comes. Walby believed that by both Public and Private Structures subordination of women continues.

Patriarchy and India

The India's civilization is 5000 years old. In this glorious civilization, the idea of Patriarchy is very old. In fact, in Harappan and Mohenzodaro the old relics of Male gods are found highlighting the patriarchal element. Later in Vedic period **Manusmriti** or **Manusanhita** plays very important role in suppressing women by writing rules and codes for women. It becomes tradition that Male will inherit the Property. He will have to live with his parents. But a girl has to be very obedient and needs to show her loyalty to her husband's family. She will need to produce male inheritors to extend the family in the future. In many cases, in case of death of her husband she has to sacrifice herself along with the body of her husband. Other way also till now a widow needs to follow lots of restrictions. Dowry system is as integral system of Hindu society. Although now, it is illegal but still practice is there. The parochial element is deeply embedded in Indian system.

Now-a-days, for the protection of Women, the Government of India provides many laws so that Women can enjoy equal status in the society. These laws are—Section 376 of Indian Penal Code for Custodial rape and Section 498-A for harassment and cruelty against women, Fast Track Court in certain cases, Family Court Act, 1984, Apart from these, there are many laws and acts passed by the government to protect women. Moreover, to see the grievances against Women, the National Commission for Women Act 1990, passed and established National Commission for Women.

Conclusion: Patriarchy is a system based on Power relation and Male domination in the society. The Patriarchy can be both public and private. The Private views of Patriarchy now become public as more and more women started to join certain services defined for man only.

Gender

The concept of gender is one of the most debatable topic now-a-days, 'Gender mainstreaming' and 'Gender Sensitization' are two of most essential topic in policy making of every country. The concepts of 'Gender' came into limelight only during mid-twentieth century when Feminist ideologies started to play an important role in sociological order. Ann Oakley in her book "**Sex, Gender and Society (1972)**" explored for first time the word "Gender". Although, earlier also it was used, but a proper definition was not there. Simone Dee Beauvior in her book "**The Second Sex**" explains that Gender differences in the society make the man superior through his role as the bread earner. It set a hierarchical position where women become subordinate. However, while defining Gender the sociologists point out three characters essential for constructing definition of Gender.

These are: (a) Gender as a process rather than a fixed state; (b) Gender as a characteristic of social as well as individuals; (c) Gender as a system that creates differences and inequalities.

Therefore, Gender is a socially constructed term to differentiate the biological differences between men and women. The term

"Gender" indicates the differences in behaviour of men and women which are described as 'Masculine' and 'Feminine'. The term "Gender" is a socially constructed term. It defines and differentiates the roles, rights, responsibilities and obligations of Women and Men. It differentiates the Social, Political and Economic Power between Sexes. The Gender differences more often used to denote Women's oppression. Ann Oakley in her books "**Sex, Gender and Society**" written in 1972 concludes that Gender divides the role of men and women in the society to support and maintain Patriarchal Society. Simone de Beauvoir in her book "**The Second Sex**" says that Gender differences are set in hierarchical opposition.

"Gender" refers to socio-cultural definition of men and women, the way in which they will play socially acceptable roles. These are maintained by multiple structures like Family, Community, Society, Culture, Language Education, Media and Religion.

In short, Gender refers to—

- The social differences between men and women.
- Gender is a learned and enforced behaviour.
- It varies with and also within culture.
- It changes over times.

Shaping of Gender Differences

(a) **Through Process of Socialization:** The Process of Socialization when a child is born shows the differentiation in gender. The Social process of preference to Male child, the one who should control and inherit the property, who have responsibility to extend the family etc. shows the shaping up of gender differences.

(b) **Role of Patriarchy as an Ideology**: Patriarchy is an ideology or system through which men are held superior and responsible for those under their care. The system of patriarchy is so well knit in the social order that women often take front position in shaping gender difference. The "Paternalistic dominance is so deep-rooted that women themselves do not know that she is becoming a victim of societal norms.

(c) **Religion as an Identity giver and fixed:** Religion plays so very important role in defining "Gender". Religious manuscripts many times interpret the role of women only as a care giver. Her role is confined only to or sacrifices herself for the sake of her son, husband etc. Moreover, all the religious texts including "Manu Smriti" incorporated "Code of Conduct" of what not to do by women.

(d) **Exploitative Socio-economic Status of Women:** The socio-economic status of women is very much determined by the role she played in the society. Women may get special position in the society if she has the monetary power behind or with her. It is part of a system of Production, Consumption and distribution which is structured by Gender.

(e) **Role of Differentiation and Stereotyping:** A specific role of a person based on Gender is what is inculcated into the mindset of people. There is a Gender division into the functions of men and women in the society. Moreover, Women is taken as a producer of future Generation, she is a care giver thus stereotyping her role. Moreover, the language is also becoming a factor to show the Masculinity and Feminity concept.

Difference between Sex and Gender

Kamla Bhasin in her book "*Understanding Gender*" highlighted the following differences:

Sex	*Gender*
Sex is natural	Gender is socio-cultural and it is man-made.
Sex is biological. It refers to visible difference in genitalia and related differences in pro-creative function.	Gender is socio-cultural and it refers to masculine and feminine qualities, behaviour patterns, roles and responsibilities etc.

(*Contd.*)

Sex	*Gender*
Sex is constant, it remains the same everywhere.	Gender is variable; it changes from time to time, culture to culture, even family to family.
Sex cannot be changed.	Gender can be changed.

Gender Socialisation

Socialisation is a fundamental Concept which can be defined as the ways in which we learn to become a member of any group including the very large group we call community. The process of socialisation begins of the moment when are born and it continues through out our lives to the very end.

Gender Socialisation is a process through which individual can learn the gender norms of their society and come to develop an internal gender identity. This definition of gender socialisation contains two other terms "Gender norms" and "Gender identity" Gender norms are the sets of rules for what is appropriate masculine and feminine behaviour in a given culture. On the other hand, the way in which being feminine or masculine, a women or a man becomes an internalized part of the way we think about ourselves is our gender identity. Hence, the concept of gender identity is consistent with an individual approach to gender which focus on how gender operates from the inside (gender identity) out.

However, Gender Socialisation beings in all societies from the very moment we born, but in many societies, gender socialisation presumes the ability to look at next infant and give it a sex. In contemporary Anglo-European society, it means to put an infant into one of two categories, male or female.

Gender Socialisation is thus the process of educating and instructing males and females as to the norms, behaviours, values, and beliefs of groups membership.

Preparations for Gender socialisation begin even before the birth of the child.

Many of the gender differences just described are attributed to differences in socialisation, though, it is possible genetic and biological factors play some role.

It is important to keep in mind that gender differences are a combination of social and biological forces; sometimes one or the other has a larger influence, but both play a role in dictating behaviour. Gender stereotypes can be a result of gender socialisation.

In Western contexts, gender socialisation operates as a binary, or a concept that is exclusively comprised of two parts.

Gender Socialisation is the process by which males and females are informed about the norms and behaviours associated with their sex.

Theories of Gender Socialisation

Theories of Gender Socialisation help us to understand how the three main approaches of Gender Socialisation, namely individual, interactional and institutional, are closely interconnected and overlapping. Gender Socialisation can be better understood at the individual level because it helps to explain the ways in which Gender comes to be internalized by individuals. In fact, Gender Socialisation is the story of how Gender comes to be located inside individuals. Many of the theories of Gender Socialisation derived from the discipline of Psychology. Almost all these theories lay stress on individuals as a unit of analysis.

Gender becomes internalized through our interactions with those surrounding us. In Socio-logical Vocabulary the person being socilised in the target of Socialisation, on the other hand, the people, groups and institutions who are doing the act of socialising are the agents of socialisation. All the theories of gender socialisation agree with the view that interaction with our society is the central mechanism through which socialisation occurs and hence, gender socialisation can also be understood at an interactional leave.

Gender becomes interlined through the groups and institutions. Various institutions such as the family, school, and religion play vital rules in the process of gender socialisation. The role of media as an institution has also became increasingly important in contemporary Gender Socialisation understanding Gender Socialisation should employ all three of these levels at which Gender operates. In the following theories an attempt has been made to examine the process of Gender Socialisation at all three of these levels.

Theoretical Approaches to Gender Socialisation

There are several theories which attempt to explain gender socialisation. For example, social learning theory and Gender Schema Theory fall within the category of learning theories. Such theories try to understand the process by which children learn gender appropriate behaviour in the same way children learn in general on the other hand, other theories focus on gender and sexuality exclusively. For example, psychoanalytical theory emphasises the unconscious process involved in developing gender identity. In this regard, Stock Word opined that all three theories explain the process of Gender socialisation, even though evidence for some—as comprehensive, stand alone, explanatory theories is lacking.

Social Learning Theory

Social Learning theory is an out growth of the behaviourist tradition which defines learning in terms of stimulus and response. This theory is most closely related with the work of psychologist Albort Bandura.

According to this theory, children are reinforced bath positively and negatively for gender appropriate and inappropriate behaviour. For example, a young boy playing with dolls may be ignored by his father. Here, the lack of attention acts as a negative reinforcem
so that the boy eventually stops playing with dolls al
Similarly, parents might hug a young girl who cries—
serving as a positive reinforcement theory incre
the girl will cry again in the future. As such
suggests that both boys and girls learn th
is expected of them. Boys lear
'inappropriate' for boys while
consistent with being fem
learn by observing
imitating the

means to be male by observing his father whereas a young girl learns what it means to be female by observing her mother.

Social learning theorists identified specific sex-typed behaviours. Behaviour is sex typed when it is more expected and therefore, seen as appropriate when performed by one Sex, but lens expected and hence seen as inappropriate when performed by the other sex. Making a list of sex typed behaviours results in the articulation of a gender or sex role. So, sex typed behaviours are also similar to the concept of gender norms. According to Social learning theories Gender Socialisation works by rewarding children for engaging in sex typed behaviour that is consistent with their assigned sex category. Crying is a classic example of it. While a little girl may be soothed when she cries, a little boy may be told that boys do not cry. Crying is a sex typed behaviour, seen as OK for girls and hence not a punishable behaviour. But because it is seen as inappropriate behaviour for boys, the little boy may be punished on corrected for his crying behaviour.

Research has shown, for example, that parents who themselves exhibit sex stereotypical behaviours are not more likely than other parents to have children who exhibit strong sex stereo typical behaviours, thus discrediting the idea that children imitate same-sex adults. In addition, children—and especially boys—display gender appropriate behaviours even in the absence of reinforcement. Finally, evidence is mixed with regard to the extent to which parents reinforce male and female children differently. All of which suggests, critics argue, that children are more actively engaged in their socialisation than the theory acknowledges. Wharton writes, "To simply somewhat, we can say that social learning theory tends to view children (and other targets of socialisation) as lumps of clay that are modelled by their environment."

Cognitive Development Theory

Cognitive theories of Gender Socialisation offer a different perspective, emphasizing the development nature of the socialization process, as well as the active role the child plays in the construction of his or her gender identity. Lawrence Kohlberg, best known for his theory of moral development, was one of the first to apply theories of cognitive development to gender identity.

Specifically, he argued that "children's view of appropriate gender roles change as they grow older, reflecting their changing cognitive development." Younger children between the ages of five and eight tend to have the most rigid definitions of gender, and apply the most severe sanctions for violence of gender norms. As they age, however, children are able to develop more complex and flexible definitions of gender (Martin & Ruble, 2004). In general, however, Kohlberg believed that once children develop gender constancy—the recognition of themselves as male or female and the stable, unchanging nature of their gender—they become more motivated to demonstrate gender appropriate behaviour (Wharton, 2005).

Critics of Kahlberg's theory pointed to contradictory evidence—the fact that children demonstrate gender-typed behaviour as young as two or three years of age, long before they develop gender constancy—to discredit his theory failed to explain why children use gender, rather than some other construct, to organize their view of the world (Wharton, 2005).

Gender Schema Theory

In response, Sandra Bem introduced a second cognitive theory of Gender Socialization known as Gender Schema Theory. According to Bem, in cultures where distinctions between men and women are emphasize, children learn to use gender as a way to process information about the world. The cognitive structures, or gender schemas, help children organize information and maintain a sense of consistency and predictability (Stockard, 1999). For Bem, two characteristics of gender schemas are particularly noteworthy. She argues that gender schemas tend to be polarized, so that children believe "what is acceptable and appropriate for males (and *vice versa*)" (Wharton, 2005: 34). And secondly, gender schemas tend to be andocentric; that is children internalize the message that males and masculinity are the standard or norm, and are more highly valued than females and femininity (Wharton, 2005).

Psychoanalytic Theory

Psychoanalytic Theory differs from both social learning and cognitive developmental theories in two important respects; it is not a learning theory, and it suggests that some aspects of gender identity result from unconscious psychological processes, rather than more conscious process such as modelling or actively seeking information consistent with schemas. The psychoanalytic approach was founded by Sigmund Freud, but its application to gender socialization was more fully outlined in the late 1970s by Nancy Chodorow. For Chodorow, the key factor in the development of gender identity is the role of the mother as the primary caregiver. Because children spend more time with mother than fathers, Chodorow argues, their fast identification is with the feminine. Eventually, however, children need to develop a sense of themselves as separate, as individual identities. For girls, the processes is easier because by indentifying with the mother she has already learned how to be female. Boys, however, in developing a male gender identity, must fast reject their identification with the feminine. "Because, the boy knows most intimately what is feminine," Stockard (1999) writes, "he comes to define masculine as being 'not feminine'. " In the process of separation, boys often learned to devalue femininity as well. The psychoanalytic theory, like other socialization theories, has not escaped criticism. Gender scholars argue that it is difficult to verify empirically, that it reinforces gender stereotypes—that woman seek connection, whereas man prefers separation, for example—and that it places too much emphasis on the unconscious.

An understanding about the Agents of Gender Socialisation

Gender Socialisation occurs through various agents like parents, peer groups and mass media etc.

Parents as Socialization Agents

According to those who study gender using the individualist framework—gender as a characteristic of the person—parents are believed to be the most significant source of gender socialization. In one of the fast studies to document the differential treatment of male and female infants, researchers asked parents to indicate the extent to which a list of adjectives described their babies. Parents of female infants selected adjectives such as 'soft,' 'fine-featured,' 'little,' and 'inattentive' more often than parents of male infants.

Public-Private Divide

The concept of women's studies can be understood by an ideological divide between public and private spheres. In the 19th/20th centuries, the divide became highly gendered as men dominated every aspect of public spheres and women were closely associated with family and home. In the later part of the 20th century a number of social and legal policies leave promoted equal opportunities is the labour force and shared responsibility is the family. Despite this progress, inequalities and discriminations are still evident for a woman is every spheres of life.

Public and Private portrays two largely separate realms. Public activities are undertaken by individuals is a hidden society like all kinds of productive or paid work, political activities under the central of law and overall jurisdiction of the government or state. But private activities are free from any kind of state control. These activities are mainly confined to household activities. It has been found that the majority women are engaged is the private activities. Historically men acted within the public realm and have moved freely between the public and the private realm. On the other hand, women have been mostly restricted to the private activities and are subjected to the authority of men. This public-private divide is a means of discrimination between men and women.

Origin of the Concept of Public-Private Divide: The liberal thinkers are of the opinion that the origin of the public private concept lie in the writings of the social contract theory which explained the generic of the legitimacy of government and state. In such writings a new social order emerged from social contract comprised two spheres. One is public and political and the other is private and removed from politics. These spheres are regarded as gendered spheres. According to this theory, public realm is necessarily a masculine one. On the other hand, women due to their sexual embodiment are prevented from having the same political standing with men. Therefore, women are incorporated into the new social order and that is the private sphere. Feminist writers debating public-private dichotomy have undertaken historical or anthropological analysis of its origin and development. The concept of public-private has a role in the development of theories of women's subordinated status. Marxian feminists also explained women's secondary status in the public sphere. The theory of patriarchy also analysed women's subordination and her activities being confined to the four walls and hence it is private. Walby, a feminist writer, uses the concept of public-private to explain the changes in the status of women in Great Britain. According to Walby, in private patriarchy the oppression of women is based around the household and involves individual men exploit individual women. In the public form of patriarchy, the formal barriers to women's participation in paid work and politics are removed. Walby further explains, "women are no longer restricted to the domestic health, but have the whole society in which she moves and is exploited." According to Hilary Charlesworth, the public-private division excluded women from public work and lowered their status. In this case, the state, law, administration has listed women in the second category and recognizes women as second class citizen. Thus, position of women becomes inferior to men. This division keeps women away from respectable work, voting rights, property rights and many more. The state has also failed to provide security to women. Another feminist thinker Catherine Mackinnon viewed that human rights acts also emphasized on the activities related to public sphere of life. According to her, the international human rights laws deprive women from all-round development. Hence, she has suggested including all sorts of work related to private spheres along with public sphere into the laws of human rights. The domestic work of women as bearing and rearing children should be valued and acts should be there to protect them form any kind of discrimination. To bring equality between men and women the concept of public private division must be eliminated from the society.

Relevance in Today's World: In the age of globalization the concept of public-private divide becomes irrelevant. The feminist movements in different parts of the world have helped women to come out from the four walls of home and engage them in many activities along with their male counterparts. A number of acts have been passed by the international organizations to change the status of women and to protect them from any kind of violence and exploitation. For example, the General Assembly of UNO organized a convention in 1979 for eliminating all forms of discriminations against women. This treaty is known as CEDAW. Most of the members of UNO signed this treaty and passed a number of acts to protect women in their respective countries. In India also, the Government of India passed the 'Domestic Violence Act' in 2005 to protect them against any sort of violence in the domestic level. Due to all these efforts in the national and international levels women in most of the countries are participating in spheres of activities equally with their male counterpart. Thus, we have found Indira Gandhi, Margaret Thatcher, Benazir Bhutto, Corazon Aquino, Chandrika Kumaratunga and many more as the head of the State or Government.

Sexual Division of Labour

The division of labour between men and women according to gender is known as sexual division of labour. The concept of sexual division of labour emerged as a central in feminist debates and writings quite recently. From ancient time onwards it has been seen that there is division of labour between male and female both at home and society. At the beginning, the feminist writers were mainly concerned with explaining the roles of women is domestic life and insignificant role in the public domain of the society. Modernisation, urbanisation and industrialisation have brought several changes in the social and economic spheres of activities. These changes have direct impact on the roles of men and women in the society. Thus, the pattern of division of labour also changed. There is an adverse effect in the sexual division of labour and the status of women due to industrialisation. It has been seen that all the time the work done by women are treated as less important. They get less recognition of their work. Moreover, the division of labour was basically categorized on the basis of sex which was different and dependent on the social, cultural, historical and economic contact of the society and carried different meanings dependent on the contact.

The feminist writers are all over the world organized a number of researches to find the origin of this sexual division of labour. The search for social origin of the sexual division of labour is an important part of the strategy for the emancipation of women. To overcome this system, it is necessary to understand the foundation and functioning of the sexual division of labour. The sociological theorists opine that the sexual division of labour is determined biologically and hence unchangeable. According to biological determination, the sexual division is categorized on the basis of female biology and male biology. Women stay at home, give birth to children, rear them and undertake all the domestic functions. Men on the other hand, undertake all the strenuous work as a part of their biology. In traditional societies, men were engaged in agricultural production while women cared for the family and attend domestic tasks. Thus, the work done by women was not treated as "labour" but as natural work. On the other hand men's work resulted is the production of goods at services. Hence, it was productive labour. Thus, women's work categorized as biological, thus "natural" and men's work valued as "labour". The feminist writers explain this concept as the dominance of human being over the nature or dominance of male over the female. They further argue that the biologically determines concept of nature is a relationship of domination of men over women and exploitation of women. Under the capitalist system, labour is for the production of surplus value. In this system, women are defined as non-workers as they are house-wives. The labour of men is categorized as productive and therefore of value. The labour of women is not regarded as productive work and has no value. The sexual division of labour has made women dependent on men and that promotes the dominance of men over women. Certain arguments can put forward regarding the traditional concept of sexual division of labour as below:

- Sexual division of labour is a natural phenomenon. From the ancient time women give birth and rear the children. Thus, they perform light work within the four walls of home. As giving birth is a natural phenomenon, thus sexual division of labour is also a natural phenomenon.
- Patriarchal social system also contributed for sexual division of labour. In this system, males occupy the

position of the head of the family. Being the head he has the power to control over everything of the family including wife and other women.

- Traditionally women are dependent on men. This dependence has decreased their status in the family and society. Thus, men involve in productive work and women engaged in household work which is unproductive and devalued. This dependence of women also responsible for sexual division of labour.

Differences of physical structure of men and women also contributed for sexual division of labour. Traditionally, men are physically stronger and hence they can do hard labour. On the other hand, the physical structure of women limits their work neither the four walls of home nor their work is regarded as lighter work resembling to the capacity of their physique.

The feminist writers are all over the world raised voice against this sexual division of labour. This division has created differences between men and women. According to Dolla Costa, a well known feminist, "the sexual division of labour has encouraged the growth of capitalism." Marxists also criticised this system. To them, the surplus value of production should shared equally between men and women labourers, but is practice. There is exploitation and the labourers do not get their appropriate wages. Moreover, the sexual division of labour instigates women to involve in those works which are comparatively cheaper than the men's work. Most of the feminists demand for the elimination of the concept of sexual division of labour from the society. They also argue to reject the narrow definition of the concept of productivity or labour. It is necessary to recognise the labour which is spent on the "production of life". Production of life is the perennial condition of all other historical forms of productive labour, including under conditions of capitalist accumulation, it has to be defined as work and not as unconscious activity natural to women. Sexual division of labour is not only the problem of family but also a structural problem of the whole society. Hence, it is necessary to change the concept and recognise all kinds of labour done by the women, give them the appropriate wages. Then only we can hope for an egalitarian society.

MODEL QUESTIONS

A. Very Short Type Questions (1 Mark Each)

1. Who wrote the book "Theorizing Patriarchy"?
2. Define Patriarchy.
3. What do you mean by "Patriarchal Mode of production"?
4. Patriarchy sees rape as effective Political device. (Yes/No)
5. Who viewed Male Violence as a Structure?
6. What do you mean by Shadow Work?
7. What is "Patriarchal Mode of Production"?
8. According to Lerner, What is the basic Structure of Patriarchy?
9. "Women are made, they are not born"—Who said?
10. From which Greek word the term "Patriarchy" derived?
11. What do you mean by "Gender Socialisation"?
12. Who wrote the book "Das Capital"?
13. Patriarchy means "The rule of the head of the family". (Write Yes or No)
14. The influence of Patriarchy is not same everywhere. (Write Yes or No)
15. Education system may be considered as the medium of influence of Patriarchy. (Write Yes or No)
16. The Women's Movement was developed in Europe and in other parts of the world from the 18th century. (Write Yes or No)
17. In what two classes, the Gender can be classified?
18. The term 'Gender' is derived from French word 'Genese' and Greek word 'Gene'. (Write Yes or No)
19. There are three aspects of Gender study. (Write Yes or No)
20. Mention one factor of rising of the Gender politics.

B. Short type Questions (4/5 Marks for Each)

1. Tools for controlling Women's mobility.
2. Why Women are also in favour of patriarchy?
3. Write about any four patriarchal institutions of women deprivation.
4. Structure of patriarchy.

5. Define Gender.
6. Characteristics of Gender.
7. Distinction between Gender and Sex.
8. Write a short note on Patriarchy.
9. Point out the different aspects of shaping Gender Socialisation.
10. Describe the various aspects of Gender Socialisation.
11. Point out the importance of Gender Socialisation.
12. Point out the differences between Natural Gender and Socially created Gender.
13. Discuss the importance of Socialisation.
14. Discuss Sexual Division of Labour.
15. Point out the consequences of Patriarchy.
16. Find out the differences between Gender and Sex.
17. Define Gender.
18. Can Gender be altered? If so, how?
19. What do you mean by Sexual Division Labour? Is sexual division of labour natural?
20. What do you mean by Public Sphere? What is Private Sphere?

C. Essay Type Questions (10/12 Marks)

1. Write about the Development of Patriarchy through Human Civilisation.
2. Define Patriarchy. Discuss about various patriarchal institutions of Women's deprivation.
3. Discuss about the structure of patriarchy.
4. What do you mean by Gender? Distinguish between Gender and Sex.
5. Define the concept of patriarchy. Discuss various forms of patriarchal control in our society.
6. Discuss Patriarchy as an ideology and practice.
7. What are the fields that men control in patriarchal system?
8. Discuss about the system of controls over Women's sexuality in patriarchal society.
9. What do you mean by Gender socialisation. Discuss various theories of Gender Socialisation.

10. Write a note on Public Private Divide?
11. Discuss about Sexual Division of Labour.
12. How can you differentiate Public sphere from Private sphere.
13. Draw relation between Public *vs.* Private Division of Labour and Patriarchal Dominance in Society.
14. In what respects the Sexual Division of Labour is related to subordination of women in society.

Unit IV
Women's Movements

Western Women's Movement

It is said that origin of that Women's movement began during Nineteenth century. However, no one can deny Aristotle's idea of education for all and other rights which marked the first equal rights of Women. Later on, Locke's two treatises on state, enlightenment and French Revolution boost the idea of equal rights for all. In England **Marry Wollstone Craft** at that time wrote "A Vindication of the Rights of Women (1792)". At the same time Gerna Theodore Gottleeb von Hippel published his writings on "On the Civil Improvement of Women". These two writings paved the way for the emancipation of Women's rights at the later stages. It is, thus feminist movements started with Mary Wollstonecraft's writings. However, it must be needed to mention that Feminist Movements or Women's Movements or Liberalism actually nothing but a series of campaigns to reform and free women from various kinds of restraints. These reforms came under certain issues like Women's Suffrage or Political Right, reproductive rights, maternity leave, equal pay, Right to job, Protection against Domestic Violence etc.

Now, the question comes why it started in West? It is so because demand for various rights began as Women found themselves traditionally suppressed and inferior to men both physically and intellectually. The State, the Religion, the Law all suppressed the women from enjoying their rights. They did not enjoy any kind of freedom, rights to property, the future of their children, even over their own enjoyment. So, the demand to make them equal at par with men started with the writings of Mary

Wollstonecraft. The Women's movement thus started mainly in certain parts of the Western World and later on spread to other parts of the World. It was started mainly in Western Europe especially in France, Great Britain and Germany later to United States of America, Australia, New Zeland and to the Scandinavian countries. It is noteworthy to mention that these societies' shares certain key features, like—An Anglo-Sexon, Protestant culture combined with comparatively Liberal, Parliamentary Political System. This influences the Women to be more liberal and to have their rights in the political and economic arena (*Story Review*, 1997).

In the United States issue of Slavery proved to be an important as part in demanding rights of Women. It was because at an anti-slavery convention in 1840 in London female delegates from US Elizabeth Stanton and Lucretion Mott were prevented from taking their seats in discussion. This inequality angered them and fight began to have greater equality among men and women. Thus, Movement for Emancipation of Women began in most of the countries against inequality faced by women.

Origin of the Movement

In North America, Abigail Adams and Mercy Otis Warren pressed for the inclusion of Women's Emancipation in the US Constitution. However, the Feminist Movement really started from 1848 when Elizabeth Starton, Lucretia Mott and others issued a "Declaration of Independence for Women" in a Women's Convention at Seneca Falls, New York. In that Declaration, they demanded legal equality, equal opportunity for education and business, equal compensation, Right to Collect Wages and Right to Vote. These movements very rapidly spread to Europe. In Britain, a number of Pressure Groups started to appear at the same time. One of the first of such associations was under the leadership of Barbara Leigh Smith and Bersie Reyner state Parki who formed "the Ladies of Raglan Place" in 1885-59. In 1871 Denmark also had a women's association, Sweeden an Association for Married Women by 1873, Norway an association for the Promotion of Women's interests by 1884 and Finland a Women's Association in the same year.

Some of the common features of this type of Women's Organization are as follows:

(a) Most of such Organizations are formed by Middle Class Women.
(b) Inclusion of men is not debarred in these Organizations. In fact, in Britain the National Society for Women's suffrage employed J.S. Mill, Jacob Bright and other members of Parliament to present petition to parliament and to introduce regular Suffrage Bills.
(c) In most countries Radical Liberals and Socialist Politicians become allies with feminist.

The Communist also believed that to some extent Women's emancipation, Engel's "**Origin of the Family, Private Property and the State**" (1884) contributed to the understanding of the source of Women's Oppression and how it may be overthrown. Engel's book helped in the movement in demanding equal treatment, wages and employment among women. On the front of Suffrages Movement that began with Seneca Falls Convention got momentum when Finland and Norway gave women the right to Vote close to the end of nineteenth century. In 1893 New Zealand gave women the honour of Voting. In the year 1902, Australian Government gave franchise to women. In the United States Wyoming granted Women's Suffrage in 1869 and in the Utah in 1870. But, it was until first half of 20th century that it was not accepted by all. In the meantime, it becomes a well accepted fact a clear pattern for Women's Suffrage becomes visible.

In between the development that happened in other parts of the World the French Feminist movement was very slow and moderate. A Moderate Movement regarding Women's Rights was going on, but it was not very popular in the region where 'Feminism owes its Origin". The French Women got their right to vote only in 1945.

In German, on the other hand, the Cultural factors favoured Women's Movement, but due to repressive Political system, they had to wait until the political system was overthrown by Weimer Republic. However, the Social Democrats adopted the issue of Women's rights as early as in 1891, the Women's Suffrage and in

1896 right to equal way. But in practice it was all futile effort from feminist part and political motive from Socialist part.

From the point of view of literary development related to first wave Women's Movement, J.S. Mill's "**The Subjection of Women**" (1869) was translated into French, German, Swedish, Spanish. Polish and Italian. Herrick Ibsen's "**A Doll's House**" which questions institutions of Marriage become popular and stags play happened all over the World. More and more writers came forward at those times with ideas for Women's rights. Thus, international feminism took an institutional form only during 1888 when Elizabeth Stanton and Susan B. Anthony established the "International Council of Women" of which representative from all the European States came to join hands. In 1904, another Radical Feminist Organizations in the line of Women's Suffrage formed a "International Women's Suffrage Alliance" was set up in Berlin (German). However, the First World War affected the ideologies of the Movement. Although, the First Wave Women's Movement was all about Suffrage and equal political and economic rights of Women. But, Women, in true sense, get it only in 1920s when women got right to Suffrage. The fight for equality was the objective of First Wave Movement.

Second Wave Women's Movement

The Second Wave Women's Movement began in the early 1960 and ran through the late 1980s. In the United States after Women Suffrage was won in 1920 some new questions emerged regarding equality or Gender equality, Political and Economic equality, Social equality etc.

After the end of the Second World War, new ideas started to came up and beginning of the Second Wave Feminism started.

On 21st June, 1946, the United Nations established the UN Commission on the Status of Women. The objective of the body is gender equality and advancement of women. However, the origin of the Second Wave Feminism can be traced back to the period of Second World War when Women joined various Organizations. New types of Manufacturing industries, the changing concept of Nation of Fast Moving Consumer Goods (FMCG) emerged women started to become integral part of the industries. Thus creating a space for them, from the end of Second World War up to 1960, there was a lenient period in which women usually confined to domestic bliss. However, as time passes new issues like Maternity leave, Equal pay, Sexuality, family started to emerged. The slogan "The Personal in Political" became famous at that time.

The term "Second Wave Feminist Movement" refers mostly to the Radical feminism. However, the seed for their movement originated during 1940s when Simon De Beauvoir wrote **"The Second Sex"** (1949). It examined male-female relationship. It was published in United States of America in the year 1953. In the year 1963, another milestone book was published which affected the moment in very imported way. The book named "**The Feminine Mystique**" by Betty Freidan criticized women's role as homemaker and said that it slowed down their various productive talent. This book is credited for starting Second Wave Feminist, American President John F. Kenedy's movement in huts. In the meantime the Government released report on "The Status of Women", which revealed a great deal of gender inequality. The Movement grew popularity and judiciary become active in giving Women their due status and came out with "Equal Pay Act of 1963". In the year 1966, "The National Organization for Women" (NOW) was formed of which Betty Freidan was the President. By 1970s the 'NOW' had over 400 local chapters. This and other Women's Organizations pressured Government for abortions rights, Equal Pay for Women, Occupational upgradation or promotion in jobs for Women, Legal and Social barriers to education etc. During last part of 1960s on 1969 came **Kate Millet's** "sexual politics" which became a founding document for Radical Feminism. In fact "The Second Wave" movement also said to be the rise of Radical Feminist Movement.

The Movement, however, got momentum when the protest raised against Miss American Pageants in 1968 and 1969. The Redstocking, the New York Radical Feminists and other Organizations joined hands in protesting against beauty Pageant shows where women are treated as objects. This particular protest got media attention worldwide thus, and creating sense of awareness about Women's rights all over the World.

The key legislation that passed during that period includes Civil Rights Act of 1964, Roe *vs.* Wade Court decision, legalizing abortion, education amendment of 1972 etc. The prominent leaders of the movement at that time include Elizabeth Stanton, Betty Friedan, Gloria Steinen etc. In short, we can say that Second Wave Feminist Movement was successful except Equal Rights Amendment (ERA) which was not ratified. With Margaret Thatcher becoming the first Prime Minister of Britain, the Feminist Movement gained its most successful achievement. Also UN declared the Year 1975 as International Women's Year recognizing Women's need.

The end of Second Wave Feminism credited to the beginning of the Feminist Sex Workers. The Third Wave Movement is more about Women Power.

Third Wave Feminist Movement

The Third Wave Feminist Movement is raising questions about social issues, Women's Power, Confidence Building Measure etc. After getting Political and Economic equality, respect in Professional font, the Women's are now moved to some core issues of life like religious suppression against Women, Violence against Women, Human Trafficking, Body Surgery, Self-mutilation, Pornography, Media Presentation of Women etc.

With the effects of globalization or new economic development and re-distribution of Power system the third Feminist Wave diverted in various issues and Movement also became Localized, Nationalized and Globalised. The Movement began with the adoption of CEDAW (Convention on Elimination of All forms of Discrimination against Women) by the United Nations, General Assembly on 1979 creating awareness among the Women of the World. In addition to that was the UN declaration of UN decade for Women 1976-1985. This motivated the feminist and urges to develop new theories on feminism and inclusion of Women. Gender as specific issues in all categories be it education, Society, Politics, Religion etc.

It was African-American Feminist Rebecca Walker who first coined the term "Third Wave Feminism" in an article published in

"Ms Magazine" entitled "**Becoming the Third Wave**" in which she stated, "She is Third Wave Feminist and not Post-Feminism feminist".

The Third Wave Feminist Movement brings out a new kind of theoretical perspective. They redefine feminism and stereotypical gender questions. The Movement talks everything under the Sun from gender perspective. The debate over transgender issues gets momentum in this movement. Judith Butter was very much active in her writings in the book "**Gender Trouble**" (1990) and "**Bodies that matter**" (1993) about transgender issues, intersection between Gender and Sexuality. The focus rests on the issues of Structure and Society. Another significant contribution to the Third Wave Feminism in Donna Haraway's (1987) book "**Cyborg**" (1987/1991) which later on inspired "**Cyberfeminism**". The Third Wave Feminism brings up the issues like Glass Ceiling, Sexual Harassment, and Support for single mother etc.

The Third Wave Feminist Movement brings out these issues them making us especially both male and female about their Private Spaces. The Word like empowerment of Women becomes most visible in all the corridors of power.

One of the major contributions of this still going movement is introduction of notion of "**Transversal Politics**". The British Jew Nira Yuval Davis, the author of "**Gender and Nation**" (1979) coined the term to propagate the fact that Women across the world irrespective of their Ethnicity, Citizenship, Colours, Religion, needs to join together to fulfil their own interest of equality and respect. This Movement is a "Paradigm Shift" from Structuralism to Post-Structuralism theory.

Critics point out that the Third Wave Feminist Movement lacked basic objective or a cohesive good unlike first and Second Wave Feminist Movement.

Indian Women's Movement

The Women's Movement in India began as early as 19th century. History has lots of evidence where women played significant role in determining and changing Politics of the country. The Women like Maharani Laxmi Bai showcased the kind of women who can change the politics of the country. However, Women's Movement in the new sense began only during Nineteenth century with the beginning of Social Reform Movement and was shaped by Nationalistic Politics of the early Twentieth Century.

The Reform Movement in India began with the reform in Hindu society. The demand for distinction of the *Sati* System was the first form of resistance against Women's oppression, the Widow remarriage and abolition of Child Marriage become milestone in making the society aware about the rights of Women. It is need to mention here that as English education system introduced and schools and colleges were established, the Modernity started to touch the society.

The introduction of the new education system created a society which is reformed and more tolerant. Prominent revivalist like Ishwar Chandra Vidyasagar, Raja Ram Mohan Roy created a new wave of emancipation of Women.

The issue of Women's emancipation in India under the British colonial rule was closely liked with two important Movements—one, a Political Movement of challenge and resistance to imperialism and, the other, a Social Movement to reform traditional structures. The challenge of imperialist domination and the attempted imposition of an alien culture, however, compelled reformist to cleanse their own religious ideology. This led to Brahma and Arya Samaj. Parallel to it started Movement of Political awakening. The 1905 Swadeshi Movement saw the women came out in force to join hands and rejected the foreign goods, subsequently the Women's Property rights, abolition of caste system etc.

However, this need to be mentioned here that in the year 1856 when Vidyasagar first made a pamphlet regarding Widow Remarriage. It created controversy in the Hindu society.

The Act of 1856 legally permitted the widow remarriage system. Although as the social customs were very tight. Very few were came out to support that.

The issue of Child Marriage was another major breakthrough for Indian society. The reformers criticized it as bad evil of social customs. The government proposed and passes Marriage Act, 1872 which made some success regarding consensus age of marriage.

The 1874 Right of Property Act gave a widow some right over her husbands Property. Otherwise the Hindu Widows meted with injustice from her in-laws after of her husband.

Subordination of Women was very much seen among the Women of Nineteenth century. Although there were some persons like Jyoty Rao Phule (1827-1890) who was a low Caste Maharashtrian, who opposed Polygamy and Child Marriage and advocating Women's education and widow re-marriage. He was pioneered in setting up of schools in Maharashtra for the girls. At that time, another person, Rabindra Nath Tagore who transformed Shantiniketan into an institution for the regeneration and revival of Indian culture and ardent supporter of women's emancipation.

It needs to be mentioned here that Marathi and Gujarati reformers of 19th century were at the forefront of several Movement.

Pandita Ramabai was one of the leading Social Reformers of 19th century. Pandita Ramabai was a widow with a new born daughter. She faced severe hardships when her husband died. This affected her and she made an all out attack on orthodox Brahmins. She wrote a book "*Stree Dharma Neti*" which advocated Women's emancipation and attacked harmful traditional practices. She learnt English and travelled to many countries like USA, UK, Canada for studying, teaching and disseminating the knowledge of rights of Women.

Dr. Kadamvini Ganguly who was very much involved with Nationalist Movement and said to be active in case of Swadeshi Movement.

Ramkrishna Paramhamsa Dev was another who projected Women as "Kali" or superme Power.

Sarojini Naidu and Kamaladevi Chattopadhayay were two Radical Reformers before Independence of India. Both were politically active nationalist leader who believed in the self-rule and regulation of society. Both campaigned for Women's rights. During that period, another important figure of Women's Movement was Bhikaji Cama or Madam Cama. She was part of British Delegation to the International Socialist Congress at Stuttgart. She was a revolutionary activist at that time. Many Revolutionary Women leaders of later period were Sarla Devi Choudhurani, Warga Devi etc. In 1928 at Calcutta, a group of

Women students silently carried out revolutionary activity. Among them Kalpana Dutta was very active member who was arrested in the link of Chittagong bombing case and Preeti Wadekar for the same on Railway Officers W/B in 1932.

In 1927 All India Women's Conference started in India with a handful of Women. This later joined by prominent Women from all work of life.

Trends of Women's Movement in India

(i) Social Reform Movement

Scholars believe that women's movements began in India as a part of the social reform movement in the last century. In the Nineteenth century, Hindu, Parsee, Muslim, reforms took the challenges and first tried to reform their own societies in the face of such a massive criticism. Social reformers like. Rammohun Roy, Ishwar Chandra Vidyasagar, Mahadev Govind Ranade raised their voices against the prevailing religion and social customs like subjection of women. Roy was preparing agitation against *Sati* and the customs of caste inequalities. Ishwar Chandra Vidyasagar efforted a lot to establish a widow remarriage society. Similarly, advancement of women's education was also one of the most important steps in this direction. Their influence encouraged the British government to enact certain laws against the *Sati* system, permitting women to remarriage, abolishing the custom of child marriage etc.

But both Raja Rammohun Roy and Ishwar Chandra Vidyasagar approached towards social movement with the upper caste Hindu ladies of the society.

(ii) Women's Movements Regarding Dalit Section

Social reform movement brought to the widow remarriage issues that concerned Brahmin women. Mahatma Phule's Satya-Shodhok Movement was contemporary of the social reform movement of Ranade and Agarkar, yet this movement opposed Brahminism which subordinated the Shudra women and rebelled against it.

Tarabai Shinde and Pandita Rambai carried forth this tradition. Rambai began to work with reformers to educate women. Through the Arja Mahila Samaj. In India Pandita Ramabai established Sharada Sadan (Home of Wisdom) a school for widows, in Bombay. Later, Dr. Babasaheb Ambedkar continued the trend through his 'Dharmantra' and Rebellion against the established Hindu caste system. Women were participants in large numbers in this Ambedkari Movements. These women faced the struggle not only as 'women' but for democratic values and change in relations of production. Women took part in struggle for water. The traditional lives on the women's movements has rarely explicated its relationship with the movement. Through the name of Mahatma Phule is often mouthed. The women's movement is definitely not yet ready to denounce Brahminism and the Hindu order.

During the national movement, women also became more conscious and aware of their own national identity.

(iii) Role of Women during Nationalist Struggle

Women participation in agitation policies must be viewed first in terms of what is meant for the nationalist movements and second how these actions shaped the women's movements. The participation of women legitimized the Indian National Congress. Women activities validated Indian unity Swadeshi movement. Non-cooperation movement, civil disobedience movement and Satyagraha. The techniques of Satyagrahis were designed to wrest moral authority from the Roy and return it to the unarmed, non-violent subjects. Even the British understood that this method had a special appeal for women. Subhas Chandra Bose formed a women's organisation called Mahila Rashtriya Sena in the freedom struggle.

The participation of women in the freedom movement also shaped the movement for women's rights. Most importantly it legitimized their claim to a place in the government of India. In the years following the civil disobedience movement more and more women entered the professions and some men learned to work side by side with them as colleagues. But during the nationalist freedom struggle women's movement diverted towards developing national identity by incorporating the Sita Savitri, Lakshamibai model as the central theme of Indian womanhood.

At the same time, the participation of women had some clear drawbacks. Those demonstrating claimed to represent all Indian women but the number of groups involved other than upper and middle large. A few Muslim women were steadfast followers of Gandhi, many more either found it difficult to accept overtly Hindu ideological basis of his ideas or were neglected by the Congress organizers.

(iv) Women's Issues During the Gandhian Era

Its the 1920s the Gandhian movement brought back a sense of unity on the women's questions. Along with the question of untouchability and Hindu-Muslim question, Women's conditions also become a primary issue to be solved immediately. This has serious implications for the women's movement in general and the mobilization of women's issue for the larger political context. The national movement now created the largest possible space for the women to come out and participate on an issue which was ostensibly political, i.e. Political freedom. But at the same time the masses, including large number of women, were galvanized to raise their own group's issues in the process of movement in 1927. All India Women's Association was formed as the national body giving voice to some of the issues. This was the time when we have voices from women as well as from other sections for giving women the voting rights as representation in any possible government formation. Interestingly, this was also the time of suffrage movement in Europe gained its momentum. Many of the women who were in forefront in Gandhian movement later became involved in institutions all over the country. These institutions would play a major role in taking up serious social issues and mobilizing and leading movements in later years. In fact the method that Gandhi used in his struggle against the colonial state as well as in his movement against the untouchability and the question of communal conflict became hay mark of some of the movements by women quite often inspired by these women and institutions. In the seventies when women fought in Uttarakhand against the liquor vendors or against the falling of trees, their movement was characterized by the Gandhian ways of protest non-violent and arousing the moral conscience in the opponent.

(v) The Post-Independent Period and Women's Movement

Independence brought many promises and dreams for women in India the dreams of an egalitarian, just, democratic society, but after independence all the promises remained unfulfilled and patriarchy took different forms to suppress women. Though the constitutions provided any kind of discrimination on grounds of sex, no serious attempt was made to promote feminist causes. As a result there were demands for more women centric development in many parts of the country through occurring different movement is discussed as under. Now, I just mention the name of the major women's movement.

(a) Telengana Movement

Irregular land distribution system prevalent after independent period led to the militant share, cropper's movement. That is 'Telengana Movement' in the years 1948 to 1950 in Andhra Pradesh under the Marxist influenced Members of CPI. Women took active part in the strikes and rallies. The issues of domestic violence, wife beating were tackled by women's groups during the movement.

(b) Bhoodan Movement

Chipko movement, Tribal movement, Peasant movement, Student movement during the year 1955 another movement. Circulated around and distribution was initiated by Binoba Bhave and Jay Prakash Narayan in Bihar which is called Bhoodan Movement or Sarvodaya Movement. Even in this movement, women took active part in rallies. This movement spread to Uttarakhand under the leadership of Sundarlal Bahuguna. Meera Bahan and Santa Bahan were two women leaders who mobilised women are in this movement and they fought against alcoholism. This Sarvodaya movement focused on action against the manifestation of alcohol and the sellers of alcohol.

(c) Shahada Movement

Shahada Movement was started in the Dhulia district of Maharashtra area where tribal Bhill people resided. These Bhill landless labourers started the Shahada Movement against the extortionate protection of local landlords. The news of the rape of two Bhill women by the local landlord made this movement a mass movement.

(d) Formation of Shramic Sangathan in 1972

The Shramic Sangathan in the years 1972 and 1973, in order to face the drought and feminine and the extortionate practices of landlords tried to cultivate the government lands forcefully. They tried to use the strategies of *gheraos* and *satyagraha* for rallies where women went from but to mobilise men. During that period there was arising trend in domestic violence due to alcohol practices prevalent in that area. So, women groups raised the issue of anti-alcoholism and they turned to be militant one breaking the alcoholic dens and beating up the alcohollistic husbands who harms his wife.

(e) Anti Price Rise Movement

The Anti Price Rise Movement is the movement in the urban areas of Maharastra which in other words known as Shahadan movement from tribal village areas into the urban areas. In the year 1973, leaders like Mrinal Gore of Socialist Party, Ahlya Rangnekar of CPI-M formed the united women Anti Price Rise front. Its basic aim was consumer protection and the demands of essential commodities by the government. In this movement only the women started the strategies of demands starting by beating this with *lathies gherao* of MP's office and industrialists by offering them bangles.

This Anti Price Rise movement spread to Gujarat in the year 1975, in the name of Nava Nirman Movement where women took active part against Corruption, Black marketing. They used the method of organizing mock Corel where mock corrupted person effigy stand in the mock court and give the verdict against the corrupted person and punished him by hanging or burning his effigy and celebrated the new dawn. These are the different women movement that took place in India.

(vi) Women Movement Since 1975

The year 1975 which is regarded as the international women's year created a tremendous impact on women's movement in India. In the same year the progressive organisation of women was formed in Pune which challenged patriarchy the inequity based on feudal culture that rationalised it and also rose *Dalit* problems and the problems related to *Devdasis*. It saw religion a major agent of oppression. During that period, many organisations like Strimukti Sangathan, Mahila Samata Samik Dal etc. were forced and stressed against the sexual oppression of women in a way that earlier social reform on feminist group.

The Chipko Movement: Struggle for Conservation of Environment

The Chipko Movement that started in 1970 was a non-violent movement aimed at the protection and conservation of trees and forests from being destroyed. The name of the Chipko movement originated from the word 'embrace' as the villagers used to hug the trees and protect them from the wood cutters from cutting them. Chipko movement was based on the Gandhian philosophy of peaceful resistance to achieve the goals. It was the strong movement against those people, who were destroying the natural resources of the forests and disturbing the whole ecological balance.

The movement had begun in two or three villages of Uttarakhand when the Forest Department had denied permission to the villagers for the cutting of ash trees for the purpose of making agricultural tools. But ironically enough the Forest Department allotted the same area of land to a sports manufacture for commercial use. This move of the Forest Department severely angered the villagers and they raised their voice against the move. This protest very soon spread throughout the region. The movement gained momentum because the issues concerned ecological and economic exploitation of the region. The villagers asserted strongly that no forest-exploiting contrasts should be given to outsiders and that it is the local communities residing in that area who should have effective control over the natural resources of the region, like land, water and forests etc. They also demanded that the government should make available low cost materials to the small industries and ensure the development of the region without upsetting the ecological balance. This movement was the first of its kind in the country and it took up vital economic issues like landless forest workers, and minimum wages guarantees.

Another very significant and noteworthy dimension of the Chipko movement was the immense participation of women in it. In fact the Chipko movement had such a large participation of women that it came to be refereed to as the women's movement. This movement was targeted for acquiring forest land; and the authorities and people in power knew that this could be done only when the village communities residing in these regions gave way to them. Therefore, to make their job easier, the forest contractors supplied massive amounts of alcohol to the men of the village. This was done so that the men would not be able to provide stiff resistance to the forest and other authorities. The women, however, reacted staunchly against this step; along with the movement for saving the trees, they started campaigning against alcoholism and thus widened the base of the movement. This inclusion made the protest of the village women even stronger because it now included a social issue which posed as a threat to the entire village community. This movement saw victory, when the government issued a ban on the feeling of trees in the Himalayan region for fifteen years until the green cover was fully restored. Thus, the Chipko movement ended on a victory. This movement, however, was a landmark movement because it was the first of its genre in the Indian Territory; and it provided impetus and inspiration to many more such subsequent movements which emerged after it.

Anti-Arrack Movement: Women's Struggle against Liquor

While the farmer's movement was creating waves in the northern states of India, the southern part of India was experiencing a different kind of agitation. This agitation was the anti-arrack movement which has been a vital movement in the history of social movements in the country. This movement was mainly concentrated in the rural areas of the state of Andhra Pradesh. This movement was not a planned one, but rather a spontaneous mobilization of the women of the region demanding a ban on the sale of alcohol in their neighbouring regions.

The Course of the Movement

The year was 1992, and it was in the months of September and October. Some villages of Andhra Pradesh were caught up in grips of alcoholism and so the women of the village took up the responsibility to eradicate the problem from the roots. They put up amazingly strong resistance against the liquor mafias and other authorities and maintained their stand. This protestation came to be known as the anti-arrack movement in the state.

Origin

The women of a remote village of Dubatunga in Nellore district of Andhra Pradesh had enrolled in the Adult Literacy Drive on a large scale in the period of the initial 1990s. It was in one of the classes of the same that the women had complained immensely about the problem of alcoholism among the men in their households. The problem here was with a locally brewed alcohol popularly known as arrack. The problem appeared to be high in intensity and was increasingly affecting the mental and physical health of both the men and their respective families. These problems, however, were not limited to that only. Alcoholism among the men also adversely affected rural economy of the region. The men were buried under debts and used to remain absent from work. The women, thus, were the worst sufferers, as they had to look after the family, balance the households and also earn, as their alcoholic husbands were under the influence of arrack. This was not the end of it, as the women also had to put up with the ill temperament of their husbands who also indulged in wife-battering under the influence of the arrack. Thus the problem appeared much more serious because it had a number of additional dimensions to it.

The women of Nellore associated in spontaneous local initiatives to protest against the predominant problem in their region and compelled the shut down of the arrack outlet. This triumph of the women of Nellore worked as motivation for women from about 5000 villages and they too acted fast towards this end. They organised themselves, met in meetings passed resolutions for imposing prohibition on liquor and then sent them to the District Collector. As a result of such stringent efforts on the part of the rural women, the arrack auctions in the Nellore district were postponed 17 times. This antiliquor movement which had originated in Nellore eventually spread to other parts of the Andhra state.

Business of Arrack and Nexus between Crime and Politics: The Linkages

This movement against arrack was a every vital one. Not only because it led to large-scale moblization of the rural women, but because it touched upon have very imperative social, political and economics issued which hugely affected rural lives. During the course of the movement, it was revealed that the there was intense nexus between crime and politics set up around the business of arrack. Even the state government had a part in this evil web. It seemed that the state government collected huge taxes from the sale of arrack and hence was unwilling to impose a ban on the sale of the same, as it would have to suffer financially. The women of the movement brought such issues out in the open, making them explicit and evident. The women for the first time on the country openly discussed the menace of domestic violence, from which they had to suffer as the men in their families consumed arrack and indulged in physical violence with them. The anti-arrack movement which stemmed as a simple movement against alcoholism later emerged as one of the most fundamental women's movement of the country, which left its imprint on the history of social movements in India.

Prior to this movement, the women's organisations which were working against the social menaces of domestic violence, sexual abuse at work place, and public places etc. were mainly mobile among the urban middle class society. This was so because the urban middle class women were more educated than their other counterparts and hence more responsive to the problems which created havoc in their lives. Their struggle was mainly focused on securing a respectable position for women in the Indian society rising above the problems of injustice and gender inequalities. In the 1980s, the women's movements centred around issues of sexual violence both within the family and outside. This was definitely a remarkable step forward in the context of the Indian society where the private sphere is still regarded a "taboo" to be talked about or discussed in public. Thus by following such projections of problems these women's groups subsequently demanded personal and property laws based primarily on gender equality.

We need to note that these assertions by the women's movements created a new kind of awareness in the Indian society. They increased the social awareness of the people on issues related to women and their rights. Along with time, the thrust of the women's movements shifted from legal reforms to open social confrontations. However, the milestone was achieved when, the 73rd and 74th constitutional amendments were passed in response to this movement. The women had demanded equal representation for women in politics in the 1990s and thus amendments granted reservations to women at the local level political offices. Demands for extending similar reservations in the State and Central legislatures were also made and a Constitution Amendment Bill with this aim has been proposed but has not yet got full favour from the Parliament. Opposition to this Bill has come from different sections of the society, including some *Dalit* women's groups who are demanding a separate quota for the *Dalit* and OBC women within the proposed women's quota in the higher political offices.

The important campaign of the contemporary Indian Feminist Movement was against Dowry, Rape, *Sati* the important feminist movement during this period were briefly mentioned below:

(1) *Movement against Rape regarding the Rameeza Bee Case in 1978*: When the new feminist groups were formed in the late seventies, they were already familiar with the categories

of police and landlord rape, for both, especially the former, had been protested against by the Maoist movement. Moreover the issue of police rape achieved new significance in 1978. Just as feminist groups were in the process of formation. Through an incident in Hyderabad, where a woman, called Rameeza Bee, was raped by several policemen, and her rickshaw-puller husband murdered because he protested at his wife's gang rape. Following this rape and murder, twenty two thousand Hyderabadis went to the police station, laid the rickshaw puller's dead body in the station verandah, set up road blocks, cut the telephone wires stoned the building and set fire to some bicycle in the compound. Two platoons of armed police were called in to quell the crowds fray, Politicians entered the fray and the Chief Minister was gheraoed the next day by members of the opposition. In the course of the gherao the police fired on the crowd, further exacter bating the situation. The next day a Hyderabad bandh was called to protest the firing. Curfew was declared in sixteen areas and nine people were killed and eight injured by police firing in Hyderabad and Secunderabad. The agitation continued even when only be repressed after President's Rule was declared, and a commission of enquiry in the rape of Rameeza Bee and murder of her husband was appointed.

(2) Movement against Dowry regarding the *Tarbindor case*, New Delhi in 1979.
(3) Movement against *Sati* regarding the *Roop Kumari Sati case* in 1987.
(4) Movement against the *Shah Bano case* on divorce under the Muslim Personal Law in 1985.

Criticism

There are some criticisms of women movement in India. These are as follows:

(i) Women Movements in India are facing great challenges wherein they have to reconcile their traditional roles with the modern values and always had to confront a group of women in a hostile situation infused with fundamentalist religious and caste ideologies. The women produced by the Indian social are naturally affected by the dominant patriarchal ideology of our society. Moreover women are socialized in to acceptance of a culture of domination by the male.

(ii) Globalization could be regarded as another sophisticated tool that created set backs to women's movement in India. One cannot ignore the fact that women have together in local network as well as network of solidarity with movements across the globe on one hand but on the other hand it is creating a myth of beautification of the women and hereby dividing women into beauty and ugly.

(iii) Moreover, the dirty political game and fundamentalist forces also play a very important role in creating obstacles to women's Movement. Here one may refer to the *Shah Bano case*, where she was deprived of her aim only due to the inherent politics.

(iv) The Women's movement is focusing on will not come easy. India is a Vast Country with diverse population. Moreover women themselves does not belong to homogenous whole. They are divided into caste, class, religion, urban/rural grounds. Due to the diversity, different problems are faced by women residing in different regions of the country and also of different hierarchical structures of the society. This resulted into lack of networking among different women organisations which costumed into fragmented women's movement rather than a united national women's movement.

Suggestion

There are some suggestions for success of the women's movement these are discussing as follows:

(i) For the success of the women's movement women must get united with strong networking. In this regard the different media of communication should play important role to help the women's movement.

(ii) It is a recognized fact that women movement must not be perceived as powered by women alone but it must include men too for fostering gender equality and in challenging the social and political order that devalues women.

(iii) The women movement must try to aim at changing the school curriculum to make it more gender neutral so that the young generation are socialized in a gender neutral way. Without societal support and awareness, women movement will always face hurdles on its way and the most humiliating will be the inner contradiction among women due to the rigid indoctrination infused through genderization by our Societal customs.

MODEL QUESTIONS

A. Very short type questions (1 Mark for Each)

1. Which year was declared as International Women Year by UNO?
2. What do you mean by Anti Arack Moment?
3. When was Prevention of Domestic Violence against Women Act was passed?
4. Name the state where Prevention of Domestic Violence Act for Women Status in not implemented?
5. Which article of the Constitution of India provides for free and compulsory education for the children between the age group 6 to 14?
6. In which district Anti-arrack movement was started?
7. When National Commission for Women was constituted?
8. Mention 2 successes of Women Movement in India?
9. Name any 2 Women leaders in India.
10. Who wrote the book "Stree Dharma Neti"?
11. Who Projected Women as "Kali" or Supreme Power?
12. Who was Pandita Ramabai?
13. Name any two Radical reformer in Pre-independence India?
14. Who for the first time propounded the idea of "education for all and other rights"?

15. Who wrote the book "A Vindication of the Rights of Women"?
16. Who wrote "On the Civil Improvement of Women"?
17. Who wrote the book "Origin of the Family, Private Property and the State"?
18. The Communist believed in Women's emancipation. (Yes or No)
19. When Australian Government gave franchise to Women?
20. When New Zeeland gave women the honour of voting?
21. Who granted Women's suffrage in US?
22. When French Women got its Voting Right?
23. Who wrote the book "The Subjection of Women"?
24. What is International Women's Suffrage alliance?
25. What was the objective of First Wave Feminist Movement?
26. Who coined the term "Transversal Politics"?
27. Write the full form of FMCG?
28. What does Second Wave Feminist Movement Mean?
29. Who wrote the book "The Second Sex"?
30. When Simone de Beavour's book "The Second Sex" was published?
31. Who authored "The Feminine Mystique"?
32. When National Organisation of Women was formed?
33. Who was the founder President of National Organisation of Women?
34. Who wrote the book "Sexual Politics"?
35. Which year was declared by UN as International Women's Year?

B. Short type questions (4/5 Marks for Each)

1. Anti-Arrack Movement.
2. Objectives of National Policy for Women Empowerment 2001.
3. National Commission on the Status of Women, 1974.
4. Any four Provision of Indian Constitution for protection of Women's rights.
5. Gandhi and Women.
6. Extremist Group of Women.

7. Features of Women's Organisation formed during 19th Century.
8. Second Wave of Feminist Movement.
9. First Wave of Feminist Movement.
10. Third Wave of Feminist Movement.
11. Trends of Women's Movement in India.
12. Telangana Movement.
13. Bhoodan Movement.
14. Chipko Movement.
15. Identify the reason which led to the Chipko Movement.

C. Long Type Questions (10/12 Marks for Each)

1. Discuss critically about the Women's Movement in India.
2. Write a note on Women's Movement in contemporary India.
3. Which are the magic issues of women movement in India?
4. Do you think Anti Arrack movement as a Women movement? Answer briefly.
5. Examine the role of women in the freedom struggle of India.
6. What is the contribution of Mahatma Gandhi to bring women to the political field? Examine the role of women's organisation in the freedom struggle?
7. Examine the role played by women extremist group in freedom struggle of India?
8. Discuss about various trends of Women's Movement in India?
9. Critically analyse the Women's Movement in India?
10. Write a note on Western Women's Movement.
11. Write an essay on Women's Movement in India.
12. Discuss about the growth and development of the Western Feminist Movement.
13. Highlight the agenda of Women's Movement.
14. Examine the importance of Women's Movement.

Unit V
Feminist Analysis of Socio-cultural and Institutional Basis of Women's Oppression

Family as an Instrument of Women's Oppression

Family is an important agent of social institution. According to Kate Millett, family is the chief institution of Patriarchy. It is a central part of society's power structure. The Second wave feminism very much included among women the idea of freeness. The feminist believed that family is the creation of Patriarchal society. They believed that only in family women can be exploited better both overtly or covertly. Radical Feminist truly believed that family is nothing but Patriarchal institution. According to Feminist there are several forms of exploitation within the family which can be discussed as below:

(i) **Domestic Labour**: In a family there is a division of work. As women is expected to do all household duties. Delphy and Leonard argue that all the unpaid housework and childcare is done by women. Women contribute largest to the family life. Yet, it is the thankless job. Marriage is nothing but a labour contract through which men exploit women's labour and become their economic masters. Women are unpaid labours in their household Marriage and Children handicapped women and debarred them to do other kinds of jobs and to compete with men. Society is also responsible for such kinds of exploitation. Society holds women responsible is most cases if break up in the family system happened. Interestingly many belief that to make women come out of marriage and to become independent the elimination of family system is much. Other felt that man should also give responsibility in household work and that there should not be any sexual division of labour.

(ii) **Parenting and Acquisition of Sexual Identity:** It is said that family is the first educational institution for any human being. It is in family that a young children learns the values, customs and expectation's of their society. It is here that boys and girls first encounter, Patriarchal element of the society. It is through the example and admonitions of their parents that they learn their role in the as appropriate to their sex. It is in family that young children got to know their sexual identity. The radicalist very much against this concept. They believe that parenting, child rearing these all have political division. It is so because many a times it is male member of the household who decides what to do or not to do by a woman.

(iii) **Economic Dependency:** The married woman who does not have any income source has to depend on their husbands for financial matter. Moreover, it is seen that as once children arrive women even give up their lucrative career for the sake of child and family. Even when mothers do return to their work it is mainly part-time. When, according to feminist women become financially dependent on her husband it eventually took all freedom from her. As men are the bread earner for the household all the key decisions are made by him. Indeed this gave the men opportunity to women and used domestic violence as tool to keep women silent.

Conclusion: The family is of the most stable and case social institution. Family holder traditional values, stable society thus making civilized society. Feminist view of Family as weapon to exploit women is not right. Women enjoyed being married, having children and running the family. Family is not about domestic labour and sexual exploitation. It is more about love, relationship, mutual understanding and companion. A healthy society can be possible only when people enjoyed blissful domestic life.

Education as an Instrument of Women's Oppression

Education played a very important role in gender construction. Anthony Gidden feels that for male curriculum plays as important role is creating gender difference. Giddens also emphasises that school text books even perpetuate gender images. The stories photos and even morals of education many times portrays gender difference. It is seen that even is story books, like 'Grimness Stories' the girls are always portrayed as vulnerable, very much soft and stories surround in and around herself, her home, love and family. Whereas the heroes of such story books always adventure. But with the first, second and third wave feminist movement that empowered and a seated awareness among all the sections of society the education system slowly becomes more gender sensitized.

It is seen that earlier women/girls are not allowed to go to do household chores, helping their mothers, become care giver to their siblings. In India till 19th century girls were very much debarred from going to school for fear of religious and social issues. But now as people become more aware about the need for education for girls, the girls are now send for the education. Due to various gender sensitized programmes the curriculum also becomes more and more gender friendly. The earlier genders stereotyping is education system is now changing. Earlier in Indian society the books like "**Manu Smriti**" as "**Manusamhita**" debarred women from doing many things. They were confined to household duties only. However, as time passed the society in becoming more outspoken. Now-a-days it is girls who outnumbered the boys in education and in other aspects of life. Earlier subjects like home economics, cooking were seen as subjects most fitted for girls to prepare them for future mother and housewife. Science earlier was not a favourable subject for the girls. Feminist argues education as an agent of secondary socialization process that helps to enforce education. The question came as how feminism has impacted education and schooling process.

With French Revolution and Renaissance, the education for

girls get some attention. It was as early as Aristotle and Plato who gave justification for the girls education especially Aristotle who believed education can provide knowledgeable women who can produce intelligent children or future king. But, the real need for education comes during 18th century. But education at that time was gender stereotyping with home schooling, food, cooking, home economics, etiquettes as subjects. The education once become preparing ground for high society women whose main function is to accompany her husband in their parties. Later on as some extraordinary women like Madam Curie became famous, it inspired many to take unconventional subject. However, it was only when during twentieth century that with the demand from radical and liberal feminist that national curriculum was introduced in .... and made subject like science, math common for all.

Sociologist Heaton and Lawson (1996) argue that the "hidden curriculum" is a major source with example of modern family usually showcased male as dominant within the family. Picture of such will portray father as superior in family, with paper works will suited, mother always is knitting mode or doing something in kitchen, boy with bicycle and girl's with dolls. Then portraying gender differences without paying or writing anything. This hidden agenda along with its sports where is the some school girls will sum playing out bolls where boys will be allotted game like rugby, cricket showed male and female difference is the education system.

It was only in later twentieth century and in twenty first century that women come forward and join with the boys and doing gender stereotyping in society.

Religion as an Instrument of Women's Oppression

Religion unites the people; spread the message of peace and love but at the same time religion also plays a negative role in men-women relation. From the ancient time onward religion had made women a subordinate section and men as the supreme. The earliest documented religions, and some contemporary, involve deification of characteristics of the natural world. These spirits are typically, but not always, gendered. It has been proposed, since the nineteenth century, that arose out of animism, as provided personalities to animist spirits in various parts of the world, notably in the development of and literature. Polytheistic gods are also typically gendered. The earliest evidence of is the worship of the goddess Eurynome, Aten in Egypt, the teaching of in the and in Aten, and Ahura Mazda are all masculine deities, embodied only in metaphor, so masculine rather than reproductively male.

Some scholars suggest that ancient religious Goddesses have been reinterpreted to follow specific gender roles. For example, the Nordic goddess Freya first represented war and love, but after centuries, she was transformed into only representing love and a sexual behaviour. The Hindu goddess Kali is interesting because she breaks the typical gendered role of women representing love, sex, fertility and beauty because she is simultaneously the goddess of the life cycle as well as destructive war. An example of the typical female goddess is Aphrodite, who is shown as vain, simple, and beautiful. In, one entity of the Trinity, the Sun, is believed to have become incarnate as a human male. Christians believe that the other two entities in the Trinity, the Father and the Holy Spirit, have never been incarnated, hence having masculine gender rather than male sex. Islam, on the other hand, has a tradition that the name Allah, like its referent, can be allocated neither grammatical nor natural gender. Masculine pronoun for Allah is interpreted as generic.

Hindu Religion

Women's inferiority underlies the conception of an ordered society in both Hinduism and Islam. The deteriorating status of Upper caste women is apparent in the Sanskrit texts of the classical age. These texts, all written by men, include the

- Dharma sastras,
- The Sastras,
- The Epics, and
- The Puranas.

With the law books of great Hindu jurists like Manu providing the general code of behaviour, the position of Indian women reached its lowest ebb. Manu, the ancient law giver had laid down that, "... by a young girl, by a young woman, or even by an aged one, nothing must be done independently, even in her own house." "In childhood a female must be subject to her father, in youth to her husband, when her lord is dead to her sons; a woman must never be independent." All her good qualities can come only from her husband (IX. 22, 23) chaining of women throughout her life. Women are to be guarded day and night as the only means to ensure purity of the offspring. **Skund Purana** says, Should a woman still wish to perform religious rites herself, she is to wash the feet of her husband and drink the water.

The Dharma shastras—the backbone of Hindu religion treated women not as a person :

1. But as a child producing living machine whose importance lies in the fact that she produces a male child.
2. Deprived women of social and political participation and her entire personality were confined to home making.
3. The Hindu scriptures treated women as property: The concept of *Kanya Dan* is nothing but the idea of property being given to the bridegroom at the time of marriage.
4. A woman was often made to pass the chastity test.

Islam Religion

1. Islam emerged as a reform movement.
2. These reforms reflected the state of development in Arabia—The reforms tried to establish peace among the warring tribes.
3. In the process Islam tried to curb the practices that were detrimental to the interest at that point of time.
4. It provided rights to men and women according to the social conditions of the time.
5. Islamic scriptures discriminated women in the same way as other religions.
6. The women were supposed to be kept in strict *purdah.*
7. They were not only supposed to be confined to the four walls of their house but would have to cover themselves from top to toe.

8. It would be a sin if she was seen by anybody outside her family circle.

Christian Religion

Christian scriptures also look down upon women as inferior to men. "God created the universe and rested. He then created man and rested again. In a subsequent manifestation he created woman and since then neither God nor man has rested." This idea is repeated by the Bible. It states how God created man first and to overcome his loneliness he created woman out of the man's ribs. Therefore, woman occupies a secondary position. She was created to please man. The woman was an instrument of pleasure. She was treated as a toy, an object, a thing. Christianity in theory does not allow polygamy. But history is full of examples of how Christian rulers indulged in debauchery. A woman confined within the four walls of the house. Therefore, in spite of a great clamour for freedom and democracy, women could get the right to vote only in the twentieth century. In Switzerland, the so-called home of democracy, women were granted the right to vote only in 1974 and that too after a great struggle.

Even as late as in 1994 Pope John Paul II in a righteous, authoritarian apostolic letter addressed to his bishops, issued a stern veto to reassert a ban against women priests, when the Church of England ordained the first women priests in March 1994.

All religions preached some common principles for women as Tolerance, Suffering and Patience. To bear all insults heaped on them by men, ungrudgingly as the highest virtue. Any protest against it in defence of their dignity and self-respect was sinful and against the principle of religion. The low caste poor women were specially the target of lust of politically and economically powerful people. The system of *Devdasi* was unmitigated prostitution carried on in the name of God.

Thus, in all religion women occupy the subordinate position. *Sati Pratha*, *Devdasi* system, *Purdah* system, polygamy etc. are different aspects of women oppression on the basis of religion. Though these aspects of oppression are gradually removing from the society but the outlook of the society has not yet changed. In the age of globalization also lot of restrictions impose on women in the name of religion. Hence, it is necessary to re-interpret the religious scriptures and understand the traditional doctrines to find out those principles which highlight the equal status and respect for women.

Women Oppression in Economic Sphere

From the ancient time onwards women have been contributing in the economic spheres both in public and private sectors but women do not enjoy economic liberty in the true sense of the term. Their contribution for the development of a state is not recognized. They face various problems in the service sector. There is discrimination in case of promotion. Moreover, the working women face multi-dimensional problems both at home and in working places. Working women face different types of physical and mental harassment at home by the family members, the authority and colleagues in the work-place and so-called leaders of the society. Women are deprived of property rights; there is discrimination for sexual division of labour. They do not get any wages for their domestic work. They feel insecure in the work-place. Above all till now there is discrimination in employment.

Industrialization has brought large quantity of employment opportunity for men not only that every work of men used to be regarded as profitable whereas women's job was confined to home and valueless job. Due to market economy, women face discrimination and ultimately they have to depend on their family member (male) for financial purposes.

In the welfare state, through the payment of taxes, some of the necessary labour is taken off individual woman. This is an advantage to the working class as a whole, and something it fought for, although there is much evidence that the welfare state was built on the exploitation of women; especially black women. It is also in the interests of capital, in that it frees working class women to be more involved in wage labour and therefore, the production of surplus value. At different times, such services will be increased, for example, during war when workers were needed, or cutback as in the early eighties when high unemployment made women workers redundant. The provisions of the welfare state are closely connected to necessary labour and the real value of a wage. Cutting back the welfare state results in an increase in necessary labour (tasks such as nursing the sick and elderly at home), and when not associated with a wage rise is an increase in exploitation, especially of women.

State and Women Oppression

It has been found that the root cause of women oppression is patriarchal system and state is a patriarchal institution. Thus state plays a negative role in protecting women's right and liberty. The state machineries in the name of controlling terrorism or law and order situation violate women's rights. Custodial torture, custodial death and custodial rape are common in every part of the world. Women are the most vulnerable group during civil war. The state as an institution has invariably colluded with patriarchy to oppress women, and this has been done through codification of cultural identities that advantage men and disadvantage women. In the past few decades, women's and feminist movements have made great strides in advancing the rights of women. The engagement of women in international development processes following the United Nations Decade of Women (1975-85) signalled a transition for women's movements—as they began developing holistic analyses of the issues impacting on women's lives, and made connections between political, economic, social and cultural realities as well as between local, national and global spaces for organising and advocating.

But reflecting on the current state of women's rights, particularly on the African continent, gives us much to ponder on. The realities that women encounter on a daily basis include pervasive violence, economic inequality, and a struggle to survive conflict, environmental changes and a backlash in many places against the gains of recent decades. The fact that only 32 out of 54 African countries had signed the Protocol on Women's Rights in Africa by the end of 2012 is indicative of the challenges that continue to block progress towards the goal of social transformation. Some would argue that 32 signatories are a success since there is no denying the importance of ensuring that we have the necessary national, regional and global legal instruments in place to tackle gender inequality. Yet, our reflections over time have made us realize that getting progressive policies adopted is but one step in a broader process since legislation on its own does not necessarily translate into broader gender equality nor has it really transformed the daily lives of many African women. Culturally, the patriarchal *status quo* remains relatively unchanged, and requires us to confront and challenge it unequivocally—and holistically.

Feminists have formulated the term 'patriarchal state', whereby the state functions mainly in the interests of men and maintains or actively supports the oppression of women (Dahlerup, 1987; Kong and Chan, 2000). For feminists, the dominance of men in this particular arena is but one of the key characteristics of a patriarchal state. While a significant number of women now occupy important positions in government and civil society, these women are challenged by the continued dominance of the 'male discourse'. Regardless of how many women enter into the political arena, if that arena is still defined by men's perspectives, there will be few opportunities to promote women's issues.

Many times the states pass some acts regarding the dress code of women which is again discriminatory as there is no such act regarding the culture or dress code of men. For example, in November 2012 in Swaziland, policy-makers opposed the protection of women from stalking. The senators argued that stalking was part of social and cultural norms and so proscribing it would violate the culture of Swazis. One senator went even further and decried the criminalization of forced marriages saying that the custom was important as it ensured that a girl's father was able to benefit from his daughter's marriage since the girl would be given to a man who has cattle to pay the bride price (Littlejohn, 2012).

In April 2013, Uganda considered a series of extraordinary measures, including one that would see women arrested for wearing skirts above the knee in public. The proposed law would mark a return to the era of Dictator Idi Amin, who banned short skirts by decree. The government-backed bill would also see many films and television dramas banned and personal internet use closely monitored by officials. Introduced by the Ethics and Integrity Minister, a former Catholic priest, the anti-pornography bill contends that there has been an "increase in pornographic materials in the Ugandan mass media and nude dancing in the entertainment world". It proposes that anyone found guilty of abetting pornography faces a 10-million shillings (US$ 4,000) fine or a maximum of 10 years in jail, or both (AWID, 2013).

The attacks on women's bodies and freedoms even extend to slashing national budgets to deal with fiscal deficits. The effects on women are compounded. They range from increasing poverty among women, unemployment as shrinking budgets lead to job cuts in health care and education (industries where women predominate), and ultimately a situation where women suffer the consequences of the State's inability to take care of its citizens. In India too the *fatawa* of *'khap' panchayat* oppressed women and interfere in their rights and liberties time to time.

Media as an Instrument of Women's Oppression

Although the media is a pervasive and profoundly influential socializing force, parents and teachers can make a difference. Young children are especially vulnerable to the teachings of media because they do not have the critical capacity necessary to distinguish between fantasy and reality, to identify persuasive intent, or to understand irony and disregard stereotypes. The cumulative and unconscious impact of these media messages can contribute to limiting the development of a child's potential, the image and representation of women and girls in the media has long been a subject of concern. Research shows that there are many fewer females than males in almost all forms of mainstream media and those who do appear are often portrayed in very stereotypical ways.

Portrayal of women in media: In everything from advertising, television programming, newspaper and magazines, to comic books, popular music, film and video games, women and girls are more likely to be shown: in the home, performing domestic chores such as laundry or cooking; as sex objects who exist primarily to service men; as victims who cannot protect themselves and are the natural recipients of beatings, harassment, sexual assault and murder.

Men and boys are also stereotyped by the media. From GI Joe

to Rambo, masculinity is often associated with machismo, independence, competition, emotional detachment, aggression and violence. Despite the fact that men have considerably more economic and political power in society than women, these trends—although different from those which affect women and girls—are very damaging to boys.

Research tells that the more television children watch, the more likely they are to hold sexist notions about traditional male and female roles and the more likely the boys are to demonstrate aggressive behaviour.

Mass media uses stereotypical characters to make it easy for the audience to identify the good guys or gals and the bad guys or gals. It is easier to create programmes around stock characters than to develop varied personalities. Stereotypes limit our views of ourselves and others and of the reality of the world. The media construct their own version of reality. The point of view of the message presented is driven by ethical, political, economic and social standards of the producers. Characters of ten reflect a narrow range of roles.

The elderly are under-represented. Women and girls are both under represented and portrayed in a very limited set of roles. Victims of violence are usually portrayed a young and beautiful women. Visible ethnic minorities often appear in limited roles. People depicted as intelligent (especially children and adolescents) are often portrayed as unattractive as well.

Renowned poet Kishwar Naheed of Pakistan has urged both print and electronic media to play a responsible role while highlighting women issues.

She was speaking at the launch of the Pakistan Women Media Complaint Cell (PWMCC) on Thursday.

The PWMCC is a joint effort of the National Commission on the Status of Women (NCSW) and the Uks Research Centre to monitor, promote and ensure gender responsiveness within the media.

Initially, the cell will start functioning from March 1 as a trial run for three months and may be extended afterwards. The cell will be an independent body and entertain complaints from the public against print and electronic media.

"Both electronic and print media should treat women with respect, dignity and honour regardless of their profession, caste and creed," Naheed said.

She expressed displeasure at some of the media outlets which promote a negative image of a woman associated with the fashion and film industries and sensationalist newspapers that use objectionable words while reporting on women.

"The print media need to be very careful and selective while using words to highlight a woman as slight irresponsible use of a word could tarnish her image in the society," she said.

Provocative images of women's partly clothed or naked bodies are especially prevalent in advertising. Shari Graydon, former president of Canada's Media Action Média, argues that women's bodies are sexualized in advertisements in order to grab the viewer's attention. Women become sexual objects when their bodies and their sexuality are linked to products that are bought and sold.

Media activist Jean Kilbourne agrees. She notes that women's bodies are often dismembered into legs, breasts or thighs, reinforcing the message that women are objects rather than whole human beings.

Although women's sexuality is no longer a taboo subject, many researchers question whether or not the blatant sexualization of women's bodies in the media is liberating. Laurie Abraham, executive editor of *Elle* magazine, warns that the biggest problem with women's magazines is "how much we lie about sex." Those "lies" continue to perpetuate the idea that women's sexuality is subservient to men's pleasure. In her study of *Cosmopolitan* and *Playboy* magazines, for example, Nicole Krassas found that both men and women's magazines contain a single vision of female sexuality—that "women should primarily concern themselves with attracting and sexually satisfying men."

Women professionals and athletes continue to be under-represented in news coverage, and are often stereotypically portrayed when they are included.

Although there has been a steady increase in the number of women professionals over the past 20 years, most mainstream press coverage continues to rely on men as experts in the fields of business, politics and economics. Women in the news are more likely to be featured in stories about accidents, natural disasters, or domestic violence than in stories about their professional abilities or expertise.

Women in politics are similarly sidelined. Canadian journalist Jenn Goddu studied newspaper and magazine coverage of three women's lobby groups over a 15-year period. She discovered that journalists tend to focus on the domestic aspects of the politically active woman's life (such as "details about the high heels stashed in her bag, her habit of napping in the early evening, and her lack of concern about whether or not she is considered ladylike" rather than her position on the issues.

Quebec political analyst Denis Monière uncovered similar patterns. In 1998, Monière analysed 83 late evening newscasts on three national networks—the Canadian Broadcasting Corporation, Radio-Canada (the French-language public broadcaster) and TVA. He observed that women's views were solicited mainly in the framework of "average citizens" and rarely as experts, and that political or economic success stories were overwhelmingly masculine.

Inadequate women's coverage seems to be a worldwide phenomenon. In 2006 the Association of Women Journalists (Association des femmes journalists—AFJ) studied news coverage of women and women's issues in 70 countries. It reported that only 17 per cent of stories quote women; one in 14 women was presented as a victim (compared to one in 21 men) and one in five women was shown in the context of her family (compared to one in 16 men).

Professor Caryl Rivers notes that politically active women are often disparaged and stereotyped by the media. When Hillary Clinton was still first lady, she was referred to as a "witch" or "witchlike" at least 50 times in the press. Rivers writes, "male political figures may be called mean and nasty names, but those words don't usually reflect superstition and dread. Did the press ever call Presidents Carter, Reagan, Bush, or Clinton warlocks?"

Women athletes are also given short shrift in the media. Margaret Carlisle Duncan and Michael Messner studied sports coverage on three network affiliates in Los Angeles. They report that only nine per cent of airtime was devoted to women's sports, in contrast to the 88 per cent devoted to male athletes. Female athletes fared even worse on ESPN's national sports show *Sports Centre*, where they occupied just over two per cent of airtime.

Duncan notes that commentators (97 per cent of whom are men) use different language when they talk about female athletes. Where men are described as "big," "strong," "brilliant," "gutsy" and "aggressive," women are more often referred to as "weary," "fatigued," "frustrated," "panicked," "vulnerable" and "choking." Commentators are also twice as likely to call men by their last names only, and three times as likely to call women by their first names only. Duncan argues that this "reduces female athletes to the role of children, while giving adult status to white male athletes."

The Prix Déméritas (Brickbat Prize) for sexist reporting was awarded by Quebec's *Gazette des femmes* to the journalists who covered the 2000 International Women's Tennis Cup. The *Gazette des femmes* noted in particular the journalists' keen interest in any of the athletes' poses that could be seen as suggestive, as well as the excessive attention accorded Anna Kournikova—for her beauty rather than her game.

Media images of women in sports are also very different from the familiar pictures of male athletes in action. Female athletes are increasingly photographed in what Professor Pat Griffin calls "hyper-sexualized poses". Griffin notes, "When it was once enough to feminize women athletes, now it is necessary to sexualize them for men. Instead of hearing, 'I am woman, hear me roar,' we are hearing 'I am hetero-sexy, watch me strip.'"

Media is expected to be act as the fourth pillar of the democracy and it is being done by many dedicated and courageous journalists too. In the recent past we witnessed a great job done by Indian electronic media to unearth the scams and corruptions cases. It may be CWG scam or 2G scam; media played a vital role to pull out the corruptions to light.

But at the same time, the incident of paid news and yellow journalism are increasing day by day. It will not be enough to say that some of so called journalists are creating news to save their job! And the GS Road molestation case in Guwahati is the result of such frustration.

Role of media is negative in representing women's issues but a true and dedicated media can play a crucial role in counteracting the impact of these messages. Helping people to understand that media construct—as opposed to reflect—reality; that they communicate implicit and explicit values; and that they can influence the way we feel and think about ourselves and the world, are vitally important lessons towards achieving a society in which women and girls are seen and treated as equal to men and boys.

Different Aspects/Dimensions of Women's Oppression in Media

(i) **Casting of women as saleable commodity:** Both electronic and print media uses women models to advertise different products of the business houses. In these advertisements the media projects women only as a commodity which is a devaluation of women community. Moreover the women do not get adequate wage for their work as model.

(ii) **Bias role of media:** Generally the media emphasize on men's power than women. In the news of rape or molestation also the media shows/publish the news in such a way that indirectly makes women responsible for all that happen to her. It will not be enough to say that some of so called journalists are creating news to save their job! And the GS Road molestation case in Guwahati is the result of such frustration.

(iii) **Insecurity of working women in media:** Many times the women working in media houses used to face harassment and feel insecure in the workplace. Rape, molestation, sexual harassment are the common problems of women workers. Sometimes they face physical assault also while collecting news from different places. Moreover their co-workers and bosses too create problems for them. The recent 'Tehelka case' is an example of such. The editor of Tehelka, Tarun Tejpal has been accused for raping and assaulting the modesty of a junior colleague in the lift.

MODEL QUESTIONS

A. Very Objective Type Questions (1 Mark for Each)

1. The family is the oldest source of Women's oppression. (Write Yes/No)
2. The Dowry Prohibition Act was adopted in 1961/1965/ 1970.
3. The Child Marriage Restrain Act was adopted in 1979/1990/2012.
4. The Sati Prevention Act was adopted in 1987/1957/2007.
5. The International Women's Day is observed on 26th January/8th March/24th October.
6. The International Human Rights Day is observed on 10th December/24th October/10th March.
7. In which year the UNO observed the year of women? (1971/1975/1985)
8. The International Day against Women's Oppression is observed on 10th December/8th March/25th November.
9. The family is the main source of Women's oppression. (Yes or No)
10. In which year the UNO observed the Women Year (1975/1985/1971)
11. The Government of India passed the Domestic Violence Act in the year (2005/2013/2000)
12. The Media is not neutral for Women. (Yes or No)
13. In modern times, the Press is controlled by the Capitalist. (Yes or No)

B. Short Type Questions (4/5 Marks Each)

1. What do you mean by Women's Oppression?
2. How far education curriculum is biased towards the Male?
3. Give four suggestions for the improvement Conditions of Women in family.
4. To what extent the State acts as an instrument of Women Oppression.
5. Point out four suggestions to improve the role of media in promoting Women Causes.

6. Give your views on Women's Oppression.
7. Mention four kinds of Women's Oppression.
8. Describe various kinds of discrimination in Workplace.
9. How does the economic system affect the life of the Women?
10. Discuss the role of media for improving the lot of Women.

C. Essay Type Questions (10/12 Marks Each)

1. Define Women's Oppression. Analyse the various Socio-cultural basis of Women's oppression.
2. What do you mean by Women's Oppression? Explain the different institutional basis of Women's oppression in India.
3. Discuss the various factors of Women's Oppression in Family.
4. Critically discuss the role of media in Women's Oppression.
5. Discuss the present scenario of Women's Oppression in India.
6. Explain Women's Oppression in Economic sphere.
7. Explain Oppression on Women by Religion.
8. Discuss how the State violates Women's rights in India.
9. Explain Women's Oppression in Education.
10. Discuss the various measures taken by the Government of India for the Preservation of Women's rights.
11. Discuss the measures initiated by the Government of India for of the Prevention of Women's Oppression.
12. Elaborate the various steps adopted at International level for the elimination of Women's Oppression.
13. In what ways the family can be considered as an institution of Women's Oppression.
14. In what respects the Present education system helps in establishing male dominance in society.
15. Critically examine the present education system and its curriculum as an institutional basis of Women's Oppression.
16. Examine religious dogmas as obstacles in the way of Women's Liberation.
17. What are the fields that men control women in Patriarchal system?

18. Discuss various forms of patriarchal control in our society.
19. Discuss about the system of central over women's sexuality in Patriarchal Society.
20. What are the social institutions through which men control and discriminate the Women class.

Annexures

Annexure I

The Protection of Women from Domestic Violence Act, 2005

No. 43 of 2005
[3rd September, 2005]

An Act to provide for more effective protection of the rights of women guaranteed under the Constitution who are victims of violence of any kind occurring within the family and for matters connected therewith or incidental thereto.

BE it enacted by Parliament in the Fifty-Sixth Year of the Republic of India as Follows:

CHAPTER I
Preliminary

1. Short title, extent and commencement.

(i) This Act may be called the Protection of Women from Domestic Violence Act, 2005.

(ii) It extends to the whole of India except the State of Jammu and Kashmir.

(iii) It shall come into force on such date as a Central Government may, by notification in the Official Gazette, appoint.

2. Definitions—In this Act, unless the context other wise requires,

(a) "aggrieved person" means any woman who is, or has been, in a domestic relationship with the respondent and who alleges to have been subjected to any act of domestic violence by the respondent.

(b) "Child" means any person below the age of eighteen years and includes any adopted, step or foster child.

(c) "Compensation order" means an order granted in terms of section 22;

(d) "Custody order" means an order granted in terms of section 21;

(e) "Domestic incident report" means a report made in the prescribed form on receipt of a complaint of domestic violence from an aggrieved person;

(f) "Domestic relationship" means a relationship between two persons who live or have, at any point of time, lived together in a shared household, when they are related by consanguinity, marriage, or through a relationship in the nature of marriage, adoption or are family members living together as a joint family.

(g) "Domestic violence" has the same meaning as assigned to it in section 3;

(h) "Dowry shall have the same meaning as assigned to it in section 2 of the Dowry Prohibition Act, 1961 (28 of 1961);

(i) "Magistrate means the Judicial Magistrate of the first class, or as the case may be, the Metropolitan Magistrate, exercising, jurisdiction under the Code of Criminal Procedure, 1973 (2 of 1974) in the area where the aggrieved person resides temporarily or otherwise or the domestic violence is alleged to have taken place;

(j) "medical facility" means such facility as may be notified by the State Government to be a medical facility for the purposes of this Act;

(k) "monetary relief" means the compensation which the Magistrate may order the respondent to pay to the aggrieved person, at any stage during the hearing of an application seeking any relief under this Act, to meet the expenses incurred and the losses suffered by the aggrieved person as a result of the domestic violence;

(l) "notification" means a notification published in the Official Gazette and the expression "notified" shall be constructed accordingly;

(m) "prescribed" means prescribed by rules made under this Act;

(n) "Protection Officer" means an officer appointed by the State Government under sub-section (1) of section 8;

(o) "Protection order" means an order made in terms of section 18;

(p) "residence order" means an order granted in terms of sub-section (1) of section 19;

(q) "respondent" means any adult male person who is, or has been, in a domestic relationship with the aggrieved person and against whom the aggrieved person has sought any relief under this Act:

Provided that an aggrieved wife or female living in a relationship in the nature of a marriage may also file a complaint against a relative of the husband or the male partner;

(r) "service provider" means an entity registered under sub-section (1) of section 10;

(s) "shared household" means a household where the person aggrieved lives or at any stage has lived in a domestic either singly or along with the respondent and includes such a household whether owned or tenanted by either jointly by the aggrieved person and the respondent, or owned or tenanted by either or them in respect of which either the aggrieved person or the respondent or both jointly or singly have any right, title, interest or equity and includes such a household which may belong to the joint family of which the respondent is a member, irrespective of whether the respondent or the aggrieved person has any right, title or interest in the shared household;

(t) "shelter home" means any shelter home as may be notified by the State Government to be a shelter home for the purpose of this Act.

CHAPTER II
Domestic Violence

3. **Definition of domestic violence**—For the purpose of this Act, any act, omission or commission or conduct of the respondent shall constitute domestic violence in case it—

(a) harms or injures or endangers the health, safety, life, limb or well-being, whether mental or physical, of the aggrieved person or tends to do so and includes causing physical abuse, sexual abuse, verbal and emotional abuse and economic abuse; or

(b) harasses, harms, injures or endangers the aggrieved person with a view to coerce her or any other person related to her to meet any unlawful demand for any dowry or other property or valuable security; or

(c) has the effect of threatening the aggrieved person or any person related to her by any conduct mentioned in clause (a) or clause (b); or

(d) otherwise injures or causes harm, whether physical or mental, to the aggrieved person.

Explanation I—For the purpose of this section—

(i) "Physical abuse" means any act or conducts which is of such a nature as the cause bodily pain, harm, or danger to life, limb, or health or impairs the health of development of the aggrieved person and includes assault, criminal intimidation and criminal force;

(ii) 'Sexual abuse' includes any conduct of sexual nature that abuse, humiliates, degrades or otherwise violates the dignity of woman;

(iii) "verbal and emotional abuse" includes—(a) insults, ridicule, humiliation, name calling and insults or ridicule specially with regard to not having a child; or a male child and (b) repeated threats to cause physical pain to any person in whom the aggrieved person is interested;

(iv) "Economic abuse" includes—

(a) deprivation of all or any economic or financial resources to which the aggrieved person is entitled under any law or custom whether payable under an order of a court or otherwise or which the aggrieved person requires out of necessity including, but not limited to, household necessities for the aggrieved person and her children, if any, stridhan property, jointly or separately owned by the aggrieved person, payment of rental related to the shared household and maintenance;

(b) disposal of household effects, any alienation of assets

whether movable or immovable, valuables, shares, securities, bonds and the like or other property in which the aggrieved person has an interest or is entitled to use by virtue of the domestic relationship or which may be reasonably required by the aggrieved person or her children or her stridhan or any other property jointly or separately held by the aggrieved person; and

(c) prohibition or restriction to continue access to resources or facilities which the aggrieved person is entitled to use or enjoy by virtue of the domestic relationship including access to the shared household.

Explanation II—For the purpose of determining whether any act, omission, commission or conduct of the respondent constitutes "domestic violence" under this section, the overall facts and circumstances of the case shall be taken into consideration.

CHAPTER III

Powers and Duties or Protection Officers, Service Providers etc.

4. Information to protection Officer and exclusion of liability of informant—(1) Any person who has reason to believe that an act of domestic violence has been, or is being, or is likely to be committed, may give information about it to the concerned Protection Officer.

(2) No liability, civil or criminal, shall be incurred by any person for giving in good faith of information for the purpose of sub-section (1).

5. Duties of police officers, service providers and Magistrate—**(a)** A police officer, Protection Officer, service provider or Magistrate who has received a complaint of domestic violence or is otherwise present at the place of an Protection Officer having jurisdiction in the area where the domestic violence took place;

(b) get the aggrieved person medically examined and forward a copy of the medical report to the Protection Officers and the police station within the local limits of which the domestic violence took place;

(c) ensure that the aggrieved person is provided shelter in a shelter home, if she so requires and forward a report of the lodging of the aggrieved person in the shelter home to the police station within the local limits of which the domestic violence took place;

(d) No suit, prosecution or other legal proceeding shall lie against any service provider or any member of the service provider who is deemed to be, acting or purporting to act under this Act, for anything which is a good faith done or intended to be done in exercise or powers or discharge of functions under this Act towards the prevention of the commission of domestic violence.

6. **Duties of shelter homes**—If an aggrieved person or on her behalf a protection Officer or a service provider requests the person in charge of the shelter home shall provide shelter to the aggrieved person in the shelter home.

7. **Duties of medical facilities**—if an aggrieved person or, on her behalf a protection officer or a service provider requests the person in charge of a medical facility to provide any medical aid to her, such person in charge of a medical facility shall provide medical aid to the aggrieved person in the medical facility.

8. **Appointment of Protection Officers**—(1) The State Government shall, by notification, appoint such number of Protection officers in each district as it may consider as it may consider necessary and shall also notify the area or areas within which a protection officer shall exercise the powers and perform the duties conferred on him by or under this Act.

(2) The Protection Officers shall as far as possible be women and shall possess such qualification and experience as may be prescribed.

(3) The terms and conditions of service of the Protection Officer and the other officers subordinate to him shall be such as may be ore scribed.

9. **Duties and function of Protection Officers**—(1) It shall be the duty of the Protection Officers—

(a) to assist the Magistrate in the discharge of the functions under this Act;

(b) to make a domestic incident report to the Magistrate, in such form and in such manner as may be prescribed, upon receipt of a complaint of domestic violence and forward copies there of to the police officer in charge of the police station within the local limits of whose jurisdiction domestic violence is alleged to have been committed and to the service providers in that area;

(c) to make an application in such form and in such manner as may be prescribed to the Magistrate, if the aggrieved person so desires, claiming relief for issuance of protection order;

(d) to ensure that the aggrieved person is provided legal aid under the Legal Services Authorities Act, 1987 (39 of 1987) and make available free of cost the prescribed from in which a complaint is to be made;

(e) to maintain a list of all service providing legal aid or counselling, shelter homes and medical facilities in a local area within the jurisdiction of the Magistrate;

(f) to make available a safe shelter home, if the aggrieved person so requires and forward a copy of his report of having lodged the aggrieved person in a shelter home to the police station and the Magistrate having jurisdiction in the area where the shelter home is situated;

(g) to get the aggrieved person medically examined, if she has sustained bodily injuries and forward a copy of the medical report to the police station and the Magistrate having jurisdiction in the area where the domestic violence is alleged to have been taken place;

(h) to ensure that the order for monetary relief under section 20 is complied with and executed, in accordance with the procedure prescribed under the Code of Criminal Procedure; 1973 (2 of 1974);

(i) to perform such other duties as many be prescribed.

(2) The protection Officer shall be under the control and supervision of Magistrate, and shall perform the duties imposed on him by the Magistrate and the Government by, or under, this Act.

10. Service providers—(1) Subject to such rules as may be made in this behalf, any voluntary association registered under the Societies Registration Act, 1860 (21 of 1860) or a company registered under the Companies Act, 1956 (1 of 1956) or any other law for the time being in force with the objective of protecting the rights and interests of women by any lawful means including providing of legal aid, medical, financial or other assistance shall register itself with the State Government as a service provider for the purpose of this Act.

(2) A service provider registered under sub-section (1) shall have the power to (a) record the domestic incident report in the prescribed form if the aggrieved person so desires and forward a copy, therefore, to the Magistrate and the protection officer having jurisdiction in the area where the domestic violence took place.

11. Duties of Government—The Central Government an every State Government, shall take all measures to ensure that—

(a) the provisions of this Act are given wide publicity through public media including the television, radio and the print media at regular in intervals;

(b) the Central Government and State Government officers including the police officers and the members of the judicial services are given periodic sensitization and awareness' training on the issues addressed by this Act;

(c) effective co-ordination between the services provided by concerned Ministries and Departments dealing with law, home affairs including law and order, health and human resources to address issues of domestic violence is established and periodicals review of the same is conducted.

(d) protocols for the various Ministries concerned with the delivery of services to women under this Act including the courts are prepared and put in place.

CHAPTER IV
Procedure for Obtaining Orders of Reliefs

12. Application to Magistrate—(1) An aggrieved person or a Protection Officers or any other person on behalf of the aggrieved person may present an application to the Magistrate seeking one or more relief's under this Act :

Provided that before passing any order on such application, the Magistrate shall take into consideration any domestic incident report received by him from the Protection Officer of the service provider.

(2) The relief sought for under sub-section (1) may include a

relief for issuance of an order for payment of compensation or damages without prejudice to the right of such person to institute a suit for compensation or damages for the injuries causes by the domestic violence committed by respondent: provided that where a decree for any amount as compensation or damages has been passed by any court in favour of the aggrieved person, the amount, if any, paid or payable in pursuance of the order made by the Magistrate under this Act shall be set off against payable under such decree and the decree shall, notwithstanding anything contained in the time being in force, be executable for the balance amount, if any, left after such set off.

(3) Every application under sub-section (1) shall be in such form and contain such particulars and may be prescribed or as nearly as possible thereto.

(4) The Magistrate shall fix the first date of hearing, which shall not ordinarily be beyond three days from the date of receipt of the application by the court.

(5) The Magistrate shall Endeavour to dispose of every application made under sub-section (1) within a period of sixty days from the date of its first hearing.

13. Service of notice—(1) A notice of the date of hearing fixed under section 12 shall be given by the Magistrate to the Protection Officer, who shall get it served by such means as may be prescribed on the respondent, and on any other person, as directed by the Magistrate within a maximum period of two days or such further reasonable time as many be allowed by the Magistrate from the date of its receipt.

(2) A declaration of service of notice made by the Protection Officer in such from as may be prescribed shall the proof that such notice was served upon the respondent and on any other person as directed by the Magistrate unless the contrary is proved.

14. Counselling—(1) The magistrate may, at any stage of the proceedings under this Act, direct the respondent or the aggrieved person, either singly or jointly, to undergo counselling with any member of a service provider who possess such qualification and experience in counselling as may be prescribed.

(2) Where the Magistrate has issued any direction under sub-section (1), he shall fix the next date of hearing of the case within a

period not exceeding two months.

15. Assistance of welfare expert—In any proceeding under this Act, the Magistrate massy secure the services of such person, preferably a woman, whether related to the aggrieved person or not, including a person engaged in promoting family welfare as he thinks fit, for the purpose of assisting him in discharging his function.

16. Proceedings to be held in camera—If the Magistrate considers that the circumstances of the case so warrant, and if either party to the proceedings so desires, he may conduct the proceedings under this Act in camera, incident of domestic violence or when the incident of domestic violence is reported to him, shall inform the aggrieved person—

(a) of her right to make an application for obtaining a relief by way of a protection order, an order for monetary relief, a custody order, a residence order, a compensation order or more than one such order under this Act;
(b) of the availability of services of service providers;
(c) of the availability of services of the Protection Officers;
(d) of her right to free legal services under the legal Services Authorities Act, 1987 (39 of 1987);
(e) of her right to file a complaint under section 498A of the Indian Penal Code (45 of 1860), wherever relevant:

Provided that nothing in this Act shall be constructed in any manner as to relieve a police officer from his duty to proceed in accordance with law upon receipt of information as to the commission of a cognizable offence.

17. Right to reside in a shared household—(1) Notwithstanding anything contained in any other law for the time being in force, every woman in a domestic relationship shall have the right to reside in the shared household, whether or not she has any right, title or beneficial interest in the same.

(2) The aggrieved person shall not be evicted or excluded from the shared household or any part of it by the respondent save in accordance with the procedure established by law.

18. Protection orders—The Magistrate may, after giving the aggrieved person and respondent an opportunity of being heard and on being *prima facie* satisfied that domestic violence has taken place or is likely to take place, pass a protection order in favour of the aggrieved person and prohibit the respondent from—

(a) Committing any act of domestic violence;
(b) aiding or abetting in the commission of acts of domestic violence;
(c) entering the place of employment of the aggrieved person or, if the person aggrieved is a child, its school or any other place frequented by the aggrieved person;
(d) attempting to communicate in any form, whatsoever, with the aggrieved person, including personal, oral or written or electronic or telephonic contact;
(e) alienating any assets, operating bank lockers or bank accounts used or held or enjoyed by both the parties, jointly by the aggrieved person and the respondent or singly by the parties or separately by them without the leave of the Magistrate;
(f) causing violence to the dependants, other relatives or any person who give the aggrieved person assistance from domestic violence; committing any other act as specified in the protection order.

19. Residence orders—(1) While disposing of an application under sub-section (1) of section 12, the Magistrate may, on being satisfied that domestic violence has taken place, pass a residence order—

(a) restraining the respondent from dispossessing or in any other manner disturbing the possession of the aggrieved person from the shared household, whether or not the respondent has a legal or equitable interest in the shared household;
(b) directing the respondent to remove himself from the shared household;
(c) restraining the respondent or any of his relatives from entering any portion of the shared household in which the aggrieved person resides;
(d) restraining the respondent from alienating or disposing of

the shared household or encumbering the same;

(e) restraining the respondent from renouncing his rights in the shared household expect with the leave of the magistrate; or

(f) directing the respondent to secure same level of alternate accommodation for the aggrieved person as enjoyed by her in the shared household or the pay rent for the same, if the circumstances so require:

Provide that no order under clause (b) shall be passed against any person who is a woman.

(2) The Magistrate may impose any additional conditions or pass any other direction which he may deem reasonably necessary to protect or to provide for the safety of the aggrieved person or any child of such aggrieved person.

(3) The Magistrate may require from the respondent to execute a bond, with or without sureties, for preventing the commission of domestic violence.

(4) An order under sub-section (3) shall be deemed to be an order under Chapter VIII of the Code of Criminal Produce, 1973 (2 of 1974) and shall be dealt with accordingly.

(5) While passing an order under sub-section (1), sub-section (2) or sub-section (3) the court may also pass an order directing the officer in charge of the nearest police station to give protection to the aggrieved person or to assist her or the person making an application on her behalf in the implementation of the order.

(6) While making an order under sub-section (1) the Magistrate may impose on the respondent obligations relating to the discharge of rent and order payments, having regard to the financial needs and resources of the parties.

(7) The Magistrate may direct the officer in charge of the police station in whose jurisdiction the Magistrate has been approached to assist in the implementation of the protection order.

(8) The Magistrate may direct the respondent to return to the possession of the aggrieved person her stridhan or any other property or valuable security to which she is entitled to.

20. Monetary reliefs—(1) While disposing of an application under sub-section (1) of section 12, the Magistrate may direct the respondent to pay monetary relief to meet the expenses incurred and losses suffered by the aggrieved person and any child of the aggrieved person as a domestic violence and such relief may include, but not limited to,

(a) The loss of earning;
(b) The medical expenses;
(c) The loss caused due to the destruction, damage or removal of any property from the control of the aggrieved person; and
(d) the maintenance for the aggrieved person as well her children, of any, including an order under or in addition to an order of maintenance under section 125 of the Code of Criminal Procedure, 1973 (2 of 1974) or any other law for the time being in force.

(2) The monetary relief granted under this section shall be adequate, fair and reasonable and consistent with the standard of living to which the aggrieved person is accustomed.

(3) The Magistrate shall have the power to order an appropriate lump sum payment or monthly payments of maintenance, as the nature and circumstances of the case may require.

(4) The Magistrate shall send a copy of the order for monetary relief made under sub-section (1), to the parties, to the application, and to the in charge of the police station within the local limits of whose jurisdiction the respondent resides.

(5) The respondent shall pay the monetary relief granted to the aggrieved person within the period specified in the order under sub-section (1).

(6) Upon the failure on the part of the respondent to make payment in terms of the order under sub-section (1), the Magistrate may direct the employer or a debtor of the respondent, to directly pay to the aggrieved person or the deposit with the court a portion of the wages or salaries or debt due to or accrued to the credit of the respondent, which amount may be adjusted towards the monetary relief payable by the respondent.

21. Custody orders—Notwithstanding anything contained in any other law for the time being in force, the Magistrate may, at any stage of hearing of the application of protection order or for any other relief under this Act grant temporary custody of any child or children to the aggrieved person or the person making an application on her behalf and specify, if necessary, the arrangements for visit of such child or children by the respondent:

Provided that if the Magistrate is of the opinion that any visit of the respondent may be harmful to the interests of the child or children, the Magistrate shall refuse to allow such visit.

22. Compensation orders—In addition to other reliefs as may be granted under this Act, the Magistrate may on an application being made by the aggrieved person, pass an order directing the respondent to pay compensation.

23. Power to grant interim and ex parte orders—(1) in any proceeding before him under this Act, the Magistrate may pass such interim order as he deems just and proper.

(2) If the Magistrate is satisfied that an application prima facie disclose that the respondent is committing, or has committed an act of domestic violence or that there is a likelihood that the respondent may commit an act of domestic violence, he may grant an *ex parte* order on the basis of the affidavit in such form, as may be prescribed, of the aggrieved person under section 18, section 19, section 20, section 21 or, as the case may be, section 22 against the respondent.

24. Court to give copies of order free of cost—The magistrate shall, in all cases where he has passed any order under this Act, order that a copy of such order, shall be given free of cost, to the parties, to the applicant, the police has been approached, and any service provider located within the local limits of domestic incident report, to that service provider.

25. During an alteration of orders—(1) A protection order made under section 18 shall be in force till the aggrieved person applies for discharge.

(2) If the Magistrate, on receipt of an application from the aggrieved person or the respondent, is satisfied that there is a changes in the circumstances requiring alternation, modification or revocation of any order made under this Act, he may, for reasons to be recorded in writing pass such order, as he may deem appropriate.

26. Relief in other suits and legal proceedings—(1) Any relief available under sections 18, 19, 20, 21 and 22 may also be sought in any legal proceeding before a civil court, family court or a criminal court, affecting the aggrieved person and the respondent whether such proceeding was initiated before or after the commencement of this Act.

(2) Any relief referred to in sub-section (1) may be sought for in addition to and along with any other relief that the aggrieved person may seek in such suit or legal proceeding before a civil or criminal court.

(3) In case any relief has been obtained by the aggrieved person in any proceeding other than a proceeding under this Act, she shall be bound to inform the Magistrate of the grant of such relief.

27. Jurisdiction—(1) The court of Judicial Magistrate of the first class or the Metropolitan Magistrate, as the case may be within the local limits of which:

(a) the person aggrieved permanently or temporarily resides or carries on business or is employed; or

(b) the respondent resides or carries on business or is employed; or

(c) the cause of action has arisen, shall be the competent court to grant a protection order and orders under this Act and to try offences under this Act.

(2) Nothing in sub-section (1) shall prevent the court from laying down its own procedure for disposal of an application under section 12 or under sub-section (2) of section 23.

28. Procedure—(1) Save as otherwise provided in this Act, all proceedings under sections 12, 18, 19, 20, 21, 22 and 23 and offences under section 31 shall be governed by the provisions of the Code of Criminal Procedure, 1973 (2 of 1974).

(2) Nothing in sub-section (1) shall prevent the court from laying down its own procedure for disposal of an application under section 12 or under sub-section (2) of section 23.

29. Appeal—There shall lie an appeal to the Court of Session within thirty days from the date on which the order made by the Magistrate is served on the aggrieved person or the respondent, as the case may be, whichever is latter.

CHAPTER V
Miscellaneous

30. Protection Officers and members of service providers to be public servants—The Protection Officers and member of service providers, while acting or purporting to act in pursuance of any of the provisions of this Act or any rules or orders made there under shall be deemed to be public servants within the meaning of section 21 of the Indian Penal Code (45 of 1860).

31. Penalty for breach of protection order by respondent—(1) A breach of protection order, or of an interim protection order, by the respondent shall be an offence under this Act and shall be punishable with imprisonment of either description for a term which may extend to one year, or with fine which may extend to twenty thousand rupees, or with both.

(2) The offence under sub-section (1) shall as far as practicable be tried by the Magistrate who had passed the order, the breach of which has been alleged to have been caused by the accused.

(3) While framing charges under sub-section (1), the Magistrate may also frame charges under section 498-A of the Indian Penal Code (45 of 1860), as the case may be, of the facts disclose the commission of an offence under those provisions.

32. Cognizance and Proof—(1) Notwithstanding anything contained in the Code of Criminal Procedure, 1973 (2 of 1974), the offence under sub-section (1) of section 31 shall be cognizable and non-bailable.

(2) Upon the sole testimony of the aggrieved person, the court may conclude that an offence under sub-section (1) of section 31 has been committed by the accused.

33. Penalty for not discharging duty by Protection Officer—If any Protection Officer fails or refuses to discharge his duties as directed by the Magistrate in the protection order without any sufficient cause, he shall be punished with imprisonment of either description for a term which may extend to one year or with fine which may extend to twenty thousand rupees, or with both.

34. Cognizance of offence committed by Protection Officers—No prosecution or other legal proceeding shall lie against the Protection Officer unless a officer authorised by it in this behalf.

35. Protection of action taken in good faith—No suit prosecution or other legal proceeding shall life against the Protection officer for any damage caused done under this Act or any rule, order made thereunder.

36. Act not in derogation of any other law—The provisions of this Act shall be in addition to, and not in derogation of the provision of any other law, for the time being in force.

37. Power of Central Government to make rules—(1) The Central Government may, by notification, make rules for carrying out the provisions of this Act.

(2) In particular, and without prejudice to the generality of the foregoing power, such rules may provide for all or the following matters, namely:

(a) The qualifications and experience which a protection officer shall possess under sub-section (2) of section 8;
(b) The terms and conditions of service of the Protection officers and the other officers subordinate to him, under sub-section (3) of section 8;
(c) The form and manner in which a domestic incident report may be made under clause (b) of sub-section (1) of section 9;
(d) The form and the manner in which an application for protection order may be made to the Magistrate under clause (c) of sub-section (1) of sub-section 9;
(e) The form in which a complain is to be filed under clause (d) of sub-section (i) of section 9;
(f) The other duties to be performed by the Protection Officer under clause (i) of sub-section (1) of section 9;
(g) The rules regulating of service providers under sub-section (1) of section 10;
(h) The form in which an application under sub-section (1) of section 12 seeking reliefs under this Act may be made and the particulars which such application shall contain under sub-section (3) of the section;
(i) The means of serving notices under sub-section (1) of section 13;
(j) The form of declaration of service of notice to be made by

the Protection Officer under sub-section (2) of section 13;

(k) The qualifications and experience in counselling which a member of the service provider shall possess under sub-section (1) of section 14;

(l) The form in which an affidavit may be filed by the aggrieved person under sub-section (2) of section 23;

(m) Any other matter which has to be, or may be, prescribed.

(3) Every rule made under this Act shall be laid, as soon as may be after it is made, before each House of Parliament, while it is in session, for a total period of thirty days which may be comprised in one session or in two or more successive session, and if, before the expiry of the session immediately following the session the successive sessions aforesaid, both Houses agree in making any modification in the rule or both Houses agree that the rule should not be made, the rule shall thereafter have effect only in such modified, such modification or annulment shall be without prejudice to the validity of anything previously done under that rule.

Annexure II

Convention on the Elimination of All Forms of Discriminations Against Women (CEDAW)

"the full and complete development of a country, the welfare of the world and the cause of peace require the maximum participation of women on equal terms with men in all fields"

CONTENTS

- Employment (Article 11)
- Health (Article 12)
- Economic and Social Benefits (Article 13)
- Rural Women (Article 14)

Part IV

- Law (Article 15)
- Marriage and Family Life (Article 16)

Part V

- Committee on the Elimination of Discrimination against Women (Article 17)
- National Reports (Article 18)
- Rules of Procedure (Article 19)
- Committee Meetings (Article 20)
- Committee Reports (Article 21)
- Role of Specialized Agencies (Article 22)

Part VI

- Effect on Other Treaties (Article 23)
- Commitment of States Parties (Article 24)
- Administration of the Convention (Articles 25-30)

Introduction

On 18 December, 1979, the Convention on the Elimination of All Forms of Discrimination against Women was adopted by the United Nations General Assembly. It entered into force as an international treaty on 3 September, 1981 after the twentieth country had ratified it. By the tenth anniversary of the Convention in 1989, almost one hundred nations have agreed to be bound by its provisions.

The Convention was the culmination of more than thirty years of work by the United Nations Commission on the Status of Women, a body established in 1946 to monitor the situation of women and to promote women's rights. The Commission's work has been instrumental in bringing to light all the areas in which women are denied equality with men. These efforts for the advancement of women have resulted in several declarations and conventions, of which the Convention on the Elimination of All Forms of Discrimination against Women is the central and most comprehensive document.

Among the international human rights treaties, the Convention takes an important place in bringing the female half of humanity into the focus of human rights concerns. The spirit of the Convention is rooted in the goals of the United Nations: to reaffirm faith in fundamental human rights, in the dignity, and worth of the human person, in the equal rights of men and women. The present document spells out the meaning of equality and how it can be achieved. In so doing, the Convention establishes not only an international bill of rights for women, but also an agenda for action by countries to guarantee the enjoyment of those rights.

In its preamble, the Convention explicitly acknowledges that "extensive discrimination against women continues to exist", and emphasizes that such discrimination "violates the principles of equality of rights and respect for human dignity." As defined in article 1, discrimination is understood as "any distinction, exclusion or restriction made on the basis of sex in the political, economic, social, cultural, civil or any other field." The Convention gives positive affirmation to the principle of equality by requiring States parties to take "all appropriate measures, including legislation, to ensure the full development and advancement of women, for the purpose of guaranteeing them the exercise and enjoyment of human rights and fundamental freedoms on a basis of equality with men" (article 3).

The agenda for equality is specified in fourteen subsequent articles. In its approach, the Convention covers three dimensions of the situation of women. Civil rights and the legal status of women are dealt with in great detail. In addition, and unlike other human rights treaties, the Convention is also concerned with the dimension of human reproduction as well as with the impact of cultural factors on gender relations.

The *legal status* of women receives the broadest attention. Concern over the basic rights of political participation has not diminished since the adoption of the Convention on the Political Rights of Women in 1952. Its provisions, therefore, are restated in article 7 of the present document, whereby women are guaranteed the rights to vote, to hold public office and to exercise public functions. This includes equal rights for women to represent their countries at the international level (article 8). The Convention on the Nationality of Married Women—adopted in 1957—is integrated under article 9 providing for the statehood of women, irrespective of their marital status. The Convention, thereby, draws attention to the fact that often women's legal status has been linked to marriage, making them dependent on their husband's nationality rather than individuals in their own right. Articles 10, 11 and 13, respectively, affirm women's rights to non-discrimination in education, employment and economic and social activities. These demands are given special emphasis with regard to the situation of rural women, whose particular struggles and vital economic contributions, as noted in article 14, warrant more attention in policy planning. Article 15 asserts the full equality of women in civil and business matters, demanding that all instruments directed at restricting women's legal capacity "shall be deemed null and void". Finally, in article 16, the Convention returns to the issue of marriage and family relations, asserting the equal rights and obligations of women and men with regard to choice of spouse, parenthood, personal rights and command over property.

Aside from civil rights issues, the Convention also devotes major attention to a most vital concern of women, namely their reproductive rights. The preamble sets the tone by stating that "the role of women in procreation should not be a basis for discrimination." The link between discrimination and women's reproductive role is a matter of recurrent concern in the Convention. For example, it advocates, in article 5, "a proper understanding of maternity as a social function", demanding fully shared responsibility for child-rearing by both sexes. Accordingly, provisions for maternity protection and child-care are proclaimed as essential rights and are incorporated into all areas of the Convention, whether dealing with employment, family law, health core or education. Society's obligation extends to offering social services, especially child-care facilities, that allow individuals to combine family responsibilities with work and participation in public life. Special measures for maternity protection are recommended and "shall not be considered discriminatory" (article 4). "The Convention also affirms women's right to reproductive choice. Notably, it is the only human rights treaty to mention family planning. States parties are obliged to include advice on family planning in the education process (article 10.h) and to develop family codes that guarantee women's rights "to decide freely and responsibly on the number and spacing of their children and to have access to the information, education and means to enable them to exercise these rights" (article 16.e).

The third general thrust of the Convention aims at enlarging our understanding of the concept of human rights, as it gives formal recognition to the influence of culture and tradition on restricting women's enjoyment of their fundamental rights. These forces take shape in stereotypes, customs and norms which give rise to the multitude of legal, political and economic constraints on the advancement of women. Noting this interrelationship, the preamble of the Convention stresses "that a change in the traditional role of men as well as the role of women in society and in the family is needed to achieve full equality of men and women". States parties are, therefore, obliged to work towards the modification of social and cultural patterns of individual conduct in order to eliminate "prejudices and customary and all other practices which are based on the idea of the inferiority or the superiority of either of the sexes or on stereotyped roles for men and women" (article 5). And Article 10.c. mandates the revision of textbooks, school programmes and teaching methods with a view to eliminating stereotyped concepts in the field of education. Finally, cultural patterns which define the public realm as a man's world and the domestic sphere as women's domain are strongly targeted in all of the Convention's provisions that affirm the equal responsibilities of both sexes in family life and their equal rights with regard to education and employment. Altogether, the Convention provides a comprehensive framework for challenging the various forces that have created and sustained discrimination based upon sex.

The implementation of the Convention is monitored by the Committee on the Elimination of Discrimination against Women (CEDAW). The Committee's mandate and the administration of the treaty are defined in the Articles 17 to 30 of the Convention. The Committee is composed of 23 experts nominated by their Governments and elected by the States parties as individuals "of high moral standing and competence in the field covered by the Convention."

At least every four years, the States parties are expected to submit a national report to the Committee, indicating the measures they have adopted to give effect to the provisions of the Convention. During its annual session, the Committee members discuss these reports with the Government representatives and explore with them areas for further action by the specific country. The Committee also makes general recommendations to the States parties on matters concerning the elimination of discrimination against women.

The full text of the Convention is set out herein.

Convention on the Elimination of All Forms of Discrimination Against Women

The States Parties to the Present Convention

Noting that the Charter of the United Nations reaffirms faith in fundamental human rights, in the dignity and worth of the human person and in the *equal rights* of men and women,

Noting that the Universal Declaration of Human Rights affirms the principle of the inadmissibility of discrimination and proclaims that all human beings are born free and equal in dignity and rights and that everyone is entitled to all the rights and freedoms set forth therein, without distinction of any kind, including distinction based on sex,

Noting that the States Parties to the International Covenants on Human Rights have the obligation to ensure the equal rights of men and women to enjoy all economic, social, cultural, civil and political rights,

Considering the international conventions concluded under

the auspices of the United Nations and the specialized agencies promoting equality of rights of men and women,

Noting also the resolutions, declarations and recommendations adopted by the United Nations and the specialized agencies promoting equality of rights of men and women,

Concerned, however, that despite these various instruments extensive discrimination against women continues to exist,

Recalling that discrimination against women violates the principles of equality of rights and respect for human dignity, is an obstacle to the participation of women, on equal terms with men, in the political, social, economic and cultural life of their countries, hampers the growth of the prosperity of society and the family and makes more difficult the full development of the potentialities of women in the service of their countries and of humanity,

Concerned that in situations of poverty women have the least access to food, health, education, training and opportunities for employment and other needs,

Convinced that the establishment of the new international economic order based on equity and justice will contribute significantly towards the promotion of equality between men and women,

Emphasizing that the eradication of apartheid, all forms of racism, racial discrimination, colonialism, neo-colonialism, aggression, foreign occupation and domination and interference in the internal affairs of States is essential to the full enjoyment of the rights of men and women,

Affirming that the strengthening of international peace and security, the relaxation of international tension, mutual co-operation among all States irrespective of their social and economic systems, general and complete disarmament, in particular nuclear disarmament under strict and effective international control, the affirmation of the principles of justice, equality and mutual benefit in relations among countries and the realization of the right of peoples under alien and colonial domination and foreign occupation to self-determination and independence, as well as respect for national sovereignty and territorial integrity, will promote social progress and development and as a consequence will contribute to the attainment of full equality between men and women,

Convinced that the full and complete development of a country, the welfare of the world and the cause of peace require the maximum participation of women on equal terms with men in all fields,

Bearing in mind the great contribution of women to the welfare of the family and to the development of society, so far not fully recognized, the social significance of maternity and the role of both parents in the family and in the upbringing of children, and aware that the role of women in procreation should not be a basis for discrimination but that the upbringing of children requires a sharing of responsibility between men and women and society as a whole,

Aware that a change in the traditional role of men as well as the role of women in society and in the family is needed to achieve full equality between men and women,

Determined to implement the principles set forth in the Declaration on the Elimination of Discrimination against Women and, for that purpose, to adopt the measures required for the elimination of such discrimination in all its forms and manifestations,

Spanish texts of which are equally authentic, shall be deposited with the Secretary-General of the United Nations.

References

Agnew, Vijay, *Women in India Politics.*

Bhagawati, Bidyut, *Sexual Division of Labour.*

Bhasin, Kamala, *Understanding Gender.*

Bhasin, Kamala, *What is Patriarchy? Kali for Women.*

Choudhury, Maitrayee, *Feminism in India.*

Devi, Radha, *Status of Women in India.*

Freedman, Jane, *Feminism.*

Gassah, L.S., *Women Empowerment Movement in North-East India.*

Gulati, Saraj, *Women and Society.*

Gupta, A.R., *Women in Hindu Society.*

Haque, Azizul, *Women and Gender Equality.*

Jana, Sewali and Sanghamitra Lahiri, *Issues in Women Studies.*

Mies, Maria, *Indian Women and Patriarchy.*

Pruthi, Raj Kumar, Rameswari Devi, Ramila Pruthi, *Indian Women Present Status and Future Prospect.*

Rahman, Zainab, *Women and Society.*

Rathod, P.B., *An Introduction to Women Studies.*

Rege, Sharmila (ed.), *Sociology of Gender.*

Research Starters, *Academic Topic Overviews.*

Saray, Sushna, *Women and Empowerment.*

Singh, B.P., *Human Rights in India.*

6 SEM TDC PSc M 2

2016 (May)

POLITICAL SCIENCE

(Major)

Course : 602

(Women's Studies)

Full Marks: 80

Pass Marks : 32

Time: 3 Hours

The figures in the margin indicate full marks for the questions.

Q. 1. Choose the correct answer/Answer/Fill in the blank of the following: **1 × 8 = 8**

(a) The book, *Vindication of the Rights of Women* was written by

(i) Mary Wollstonecraft (ii) J.S. Mill

(iii) Olympe Gouges (iv) Kate Millett

(b) Mention one demerit of the radical approach to women's studies.

(c) Mention any one measure adopted in India to protect women's right.

(d) Sex determination is a legal right.

(i) Yes (ii) No

(e) Who used the term 'gender' for the first time?

(f) "I am not permitted to construct my gender and sex willy nilly." Said by

(i) J.S. Mill (ii) Kate Millett

(iii) Michel Foucault (iv) Judith Butler

(g) The Dowry Prohibition Act was passed in

(i) 1951 (ii) 1961

(iii) 1965 (iv) 1966

(v) None of the above

(h) The convention on the Elimination of all Forms of Discrimination Against Women was adopted by .... in 1979.

Q. 2. Write on the following (within 150 words each) : $4 \times 4 = 16$

(a) Four objectives of women's studies
(b) Marxist approach to women's studies
(c) Gender socialization
(d) Devdasi system

Answer the following questions (within 500 words each)

Q. 3. Discuss the nature and scope of women's studies. $6 + 6 = 12$

Or

Trace the development of women's studies as a discipline. 12

Q. 4. Critically examine the liberal approach to women's studies. 11

Or

Evaluate the third world approaches to women's studies. What are its consequences?

Q. 5. What is patriarchy? Discuss the implication of patriarchy. 11

Or

Write a critical note on gender discrimination. 11

Q. 6. Discuss the origin and growth of the Western Women's Movement. 11

Or

Analyze the major issues of the women's movement in India in present times. 11

Q. 7. "Religion is an instrument of women's oppression." Explain. 11

Or

Discuss how family can oppress women in a society. 11